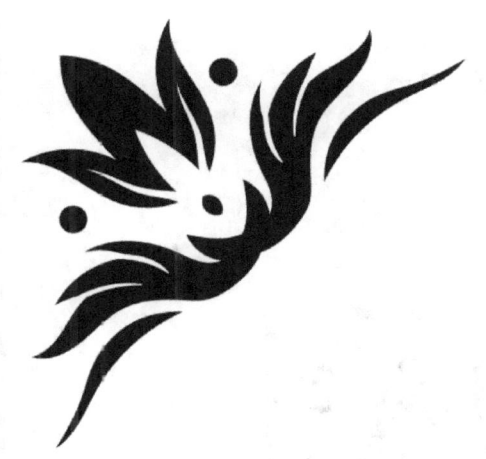

THiS BOOK BELONGS TO

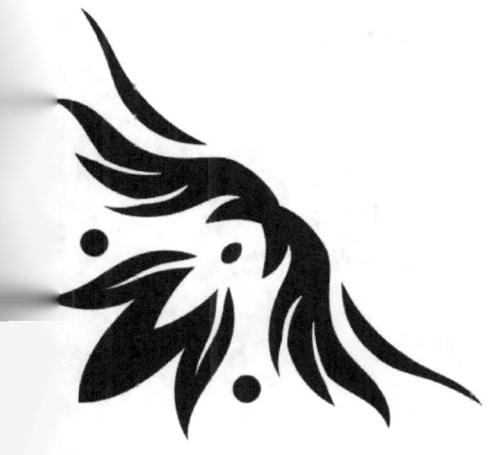
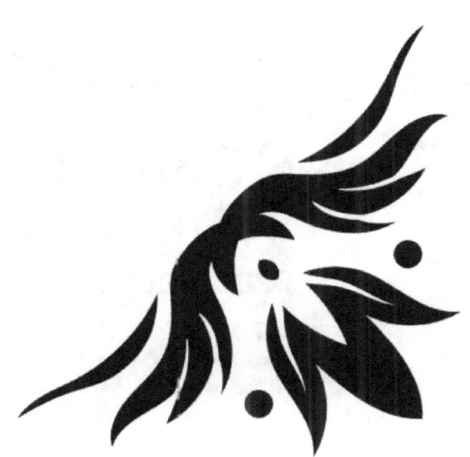

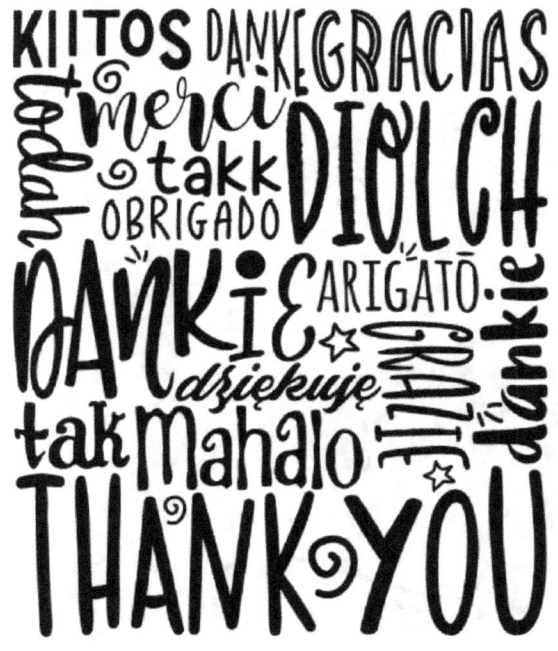

THANK YOU FOR PLACING YOUR TRUST IN ME!
I AM IMMENSELY GRATEFUL THAT YOU HAVE SELECTED
ONE OF MY BOOKS.

I KINDLY REQUEST YOU TO SHARE YOUR EXPERIENCE
AND SHOWCASE YOUR COLORED CREATIONS ON BOTH
AMAZON AND INSTAGRAM.

YOUR SUPPORT MEANS A LOT TO ME, AND I SINCERELY
APPRECIATE YOUR CONSIDERATION IN LEAVING
A REVIEW ON AMAZON.

YOUR FEEDBACK IS INCREDIBLY VALUABLE AS IT
MOTIVATES ME TO ENHANCE MY WORK AND CREATE
PRODUCTS THAT RESONATE WITH YOU.

I AM EAGERLY LOOKING FORWARD TO SEEING YOUR
BEAUTIFUL COLORING CREATIONS!

CONNECT WITH US

If you have any questions or need help, feel free to
reach out to us anytime at *support@coloringbloom.com*
Or visit our website at *coloringbloom.com*

Color Test Pages

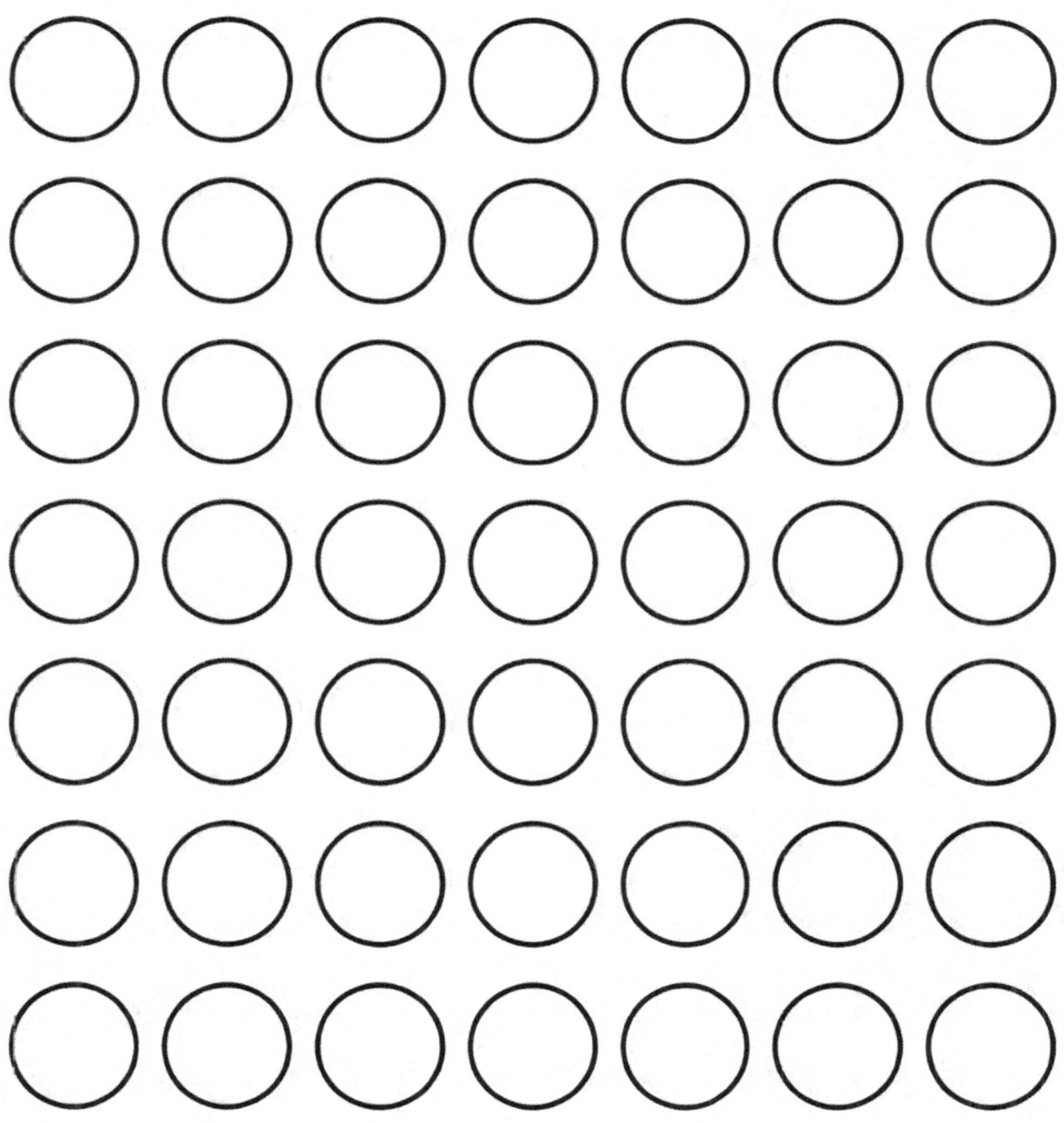

Color Test Pages

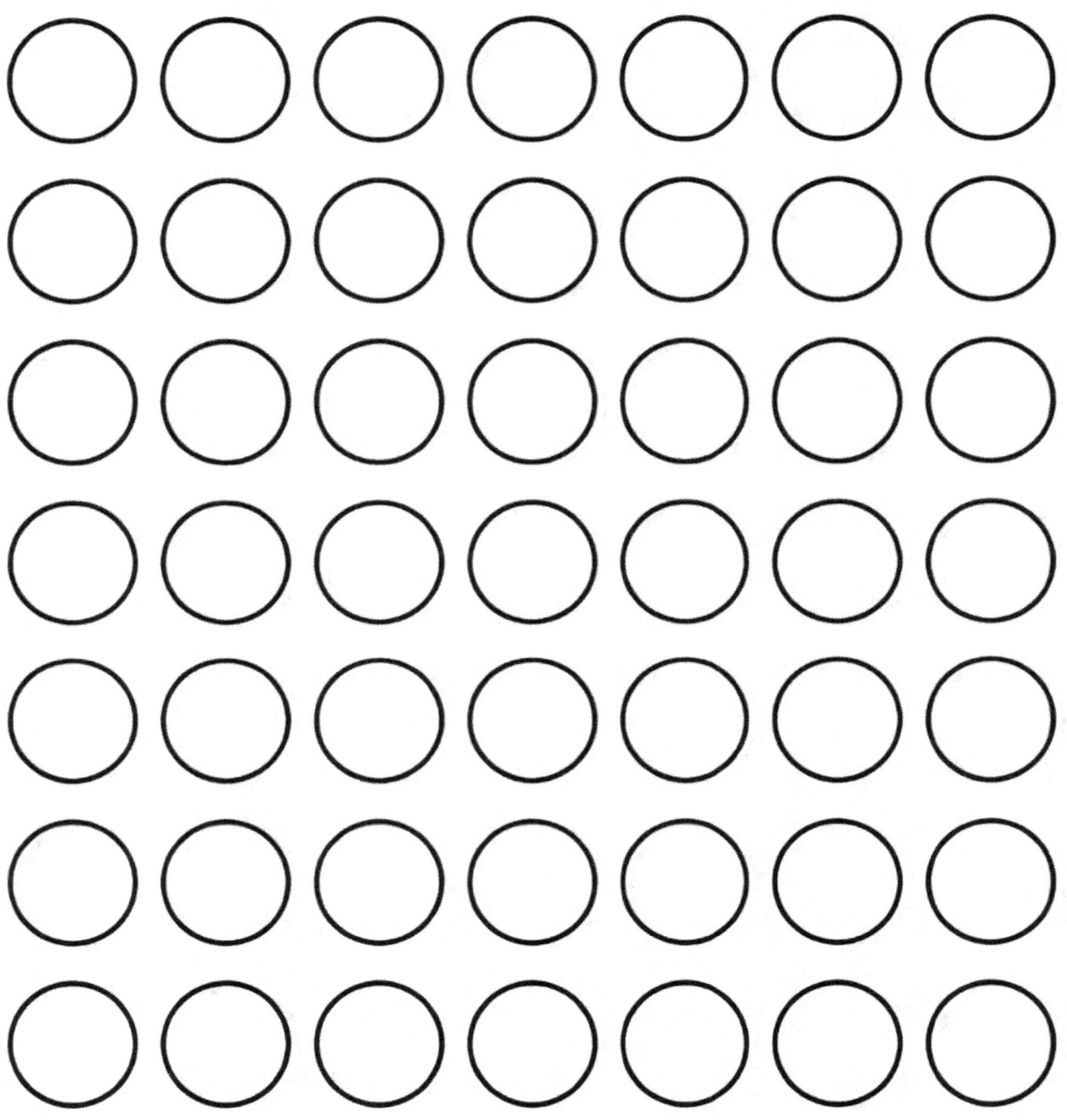

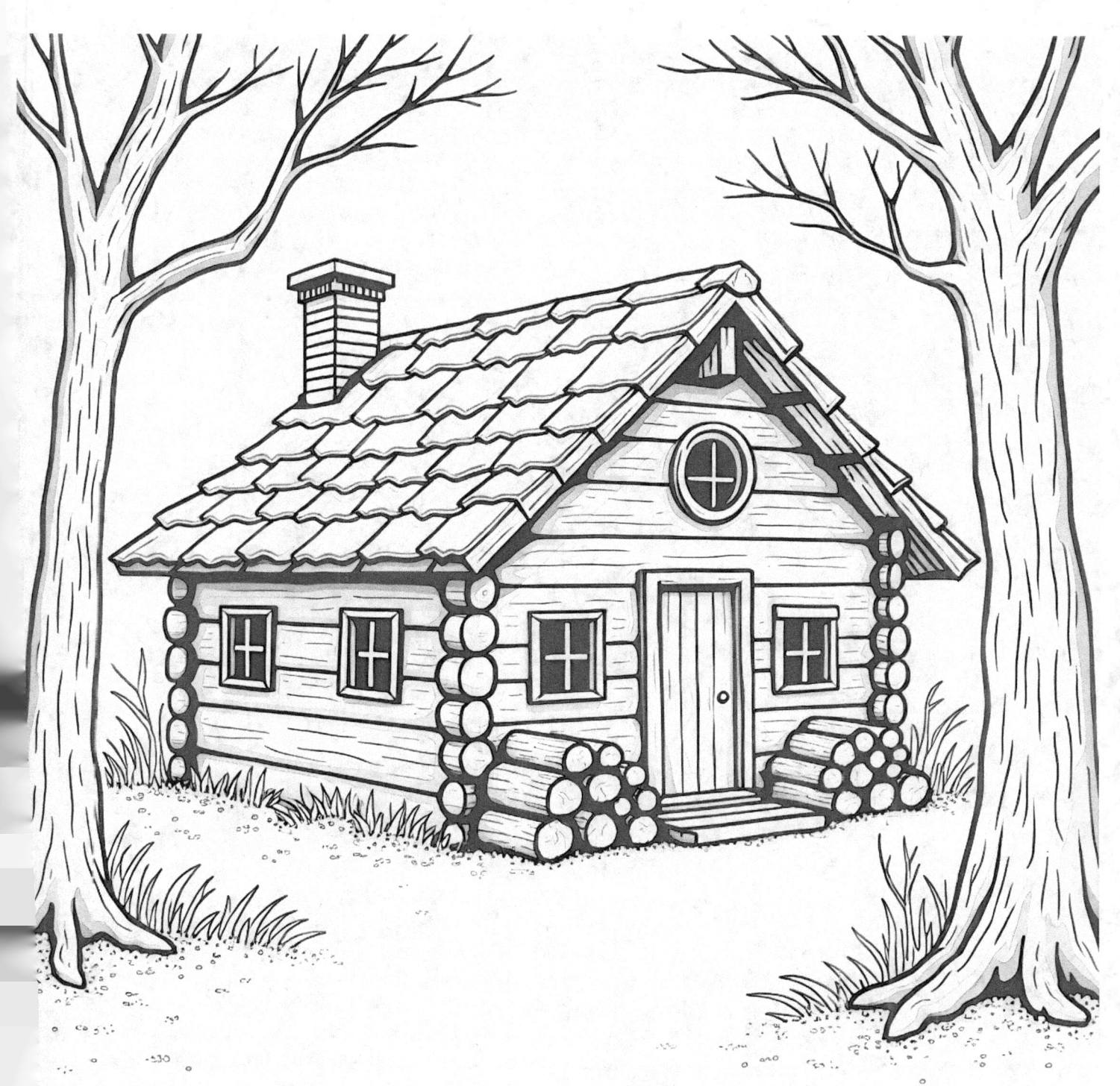

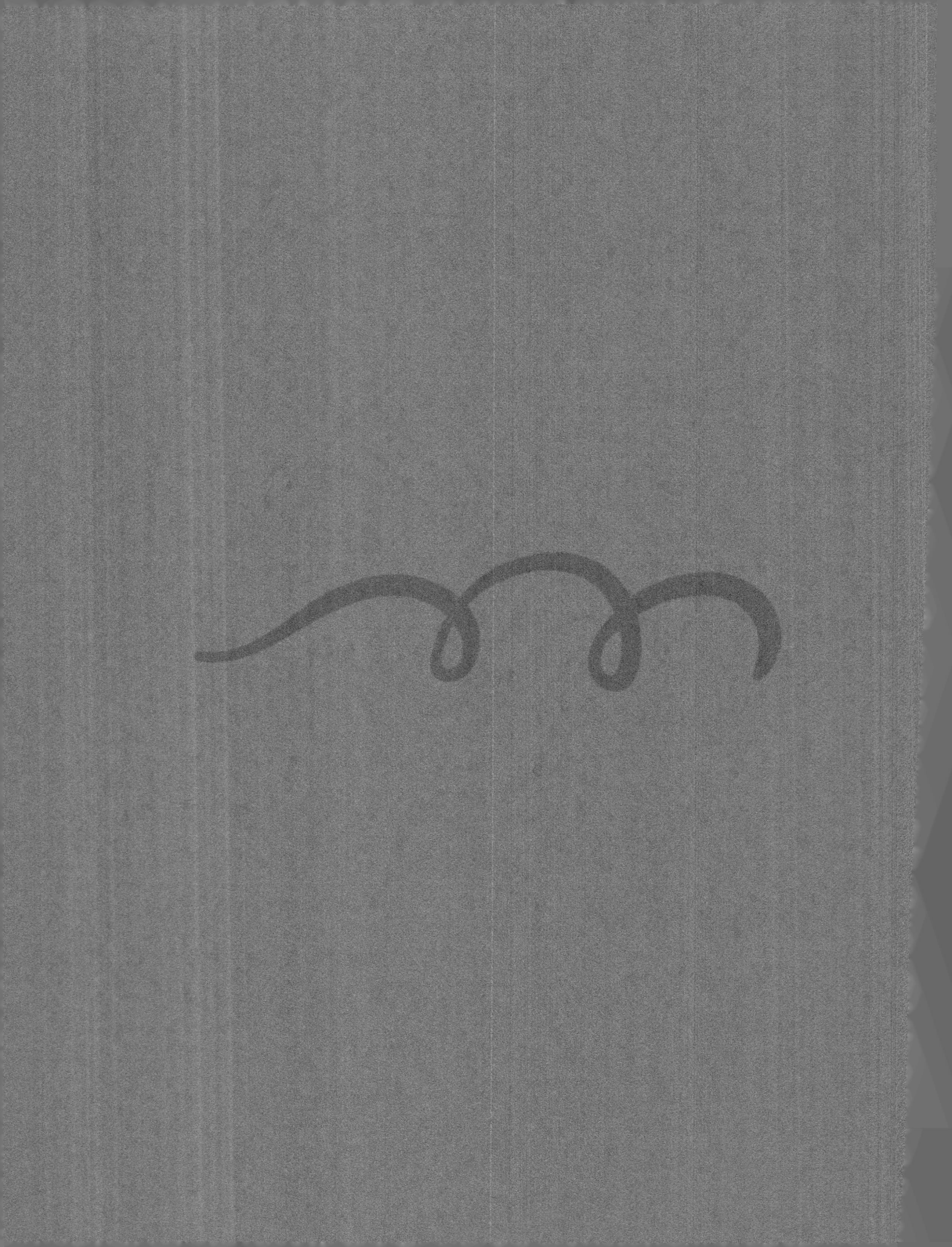

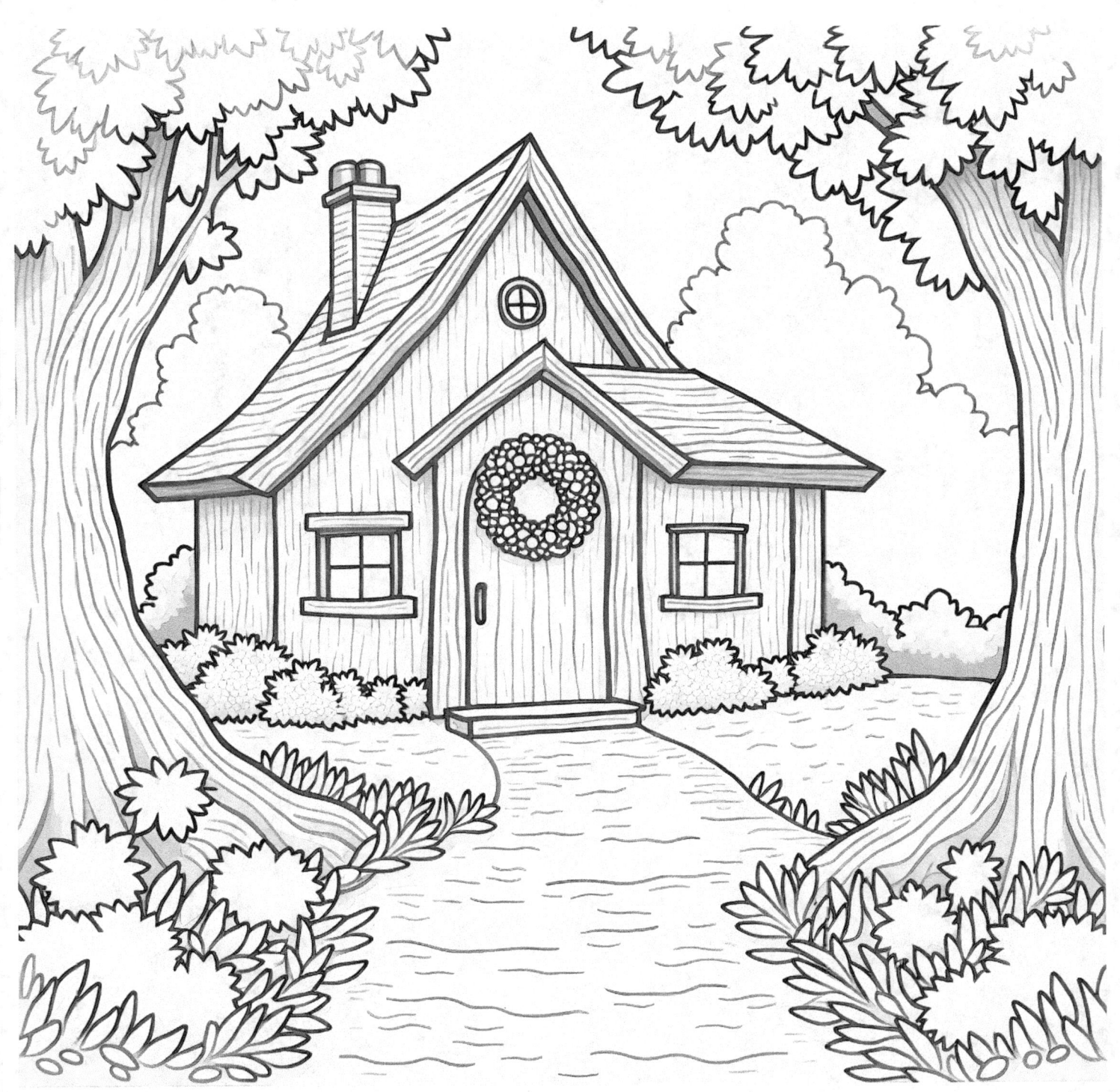

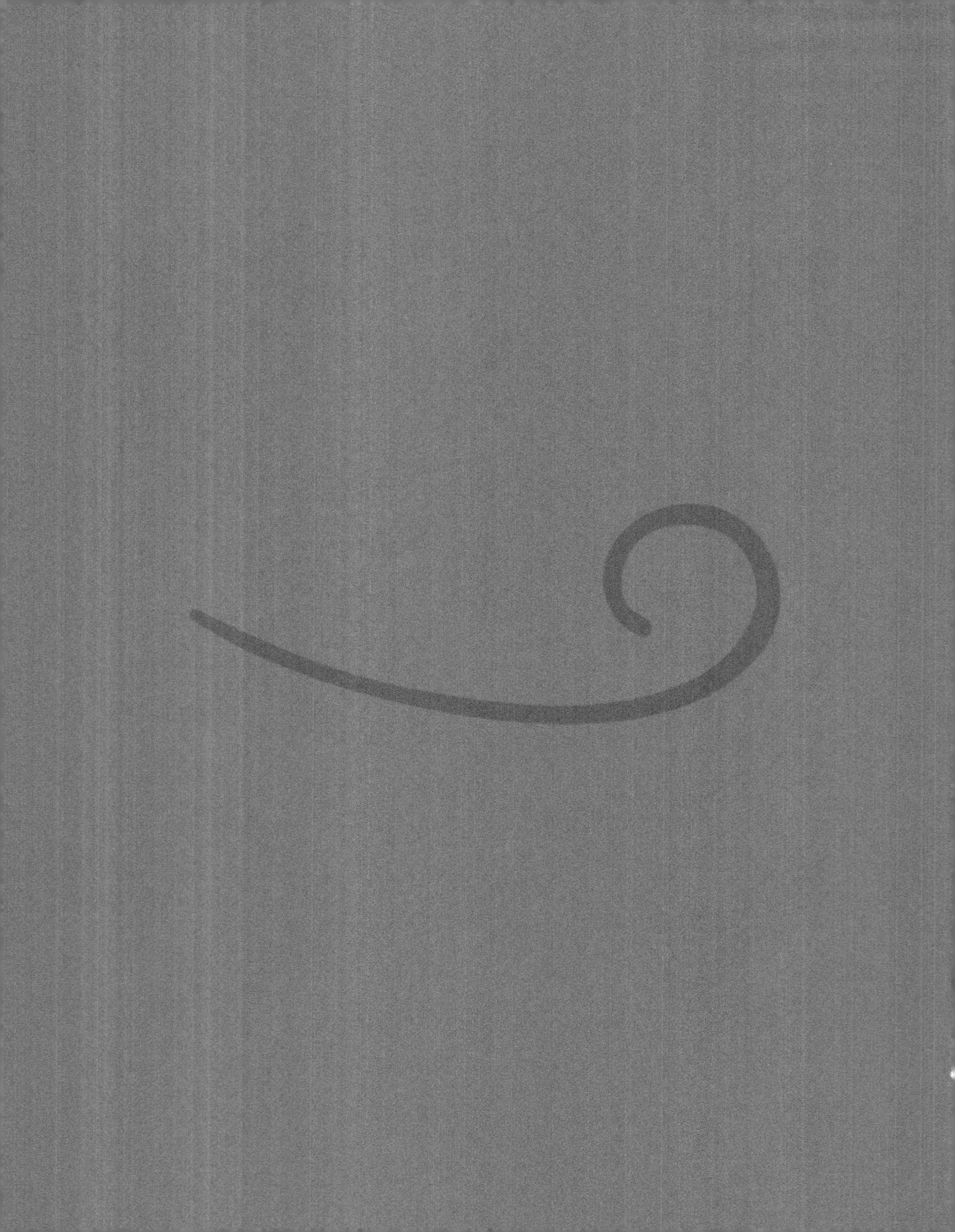

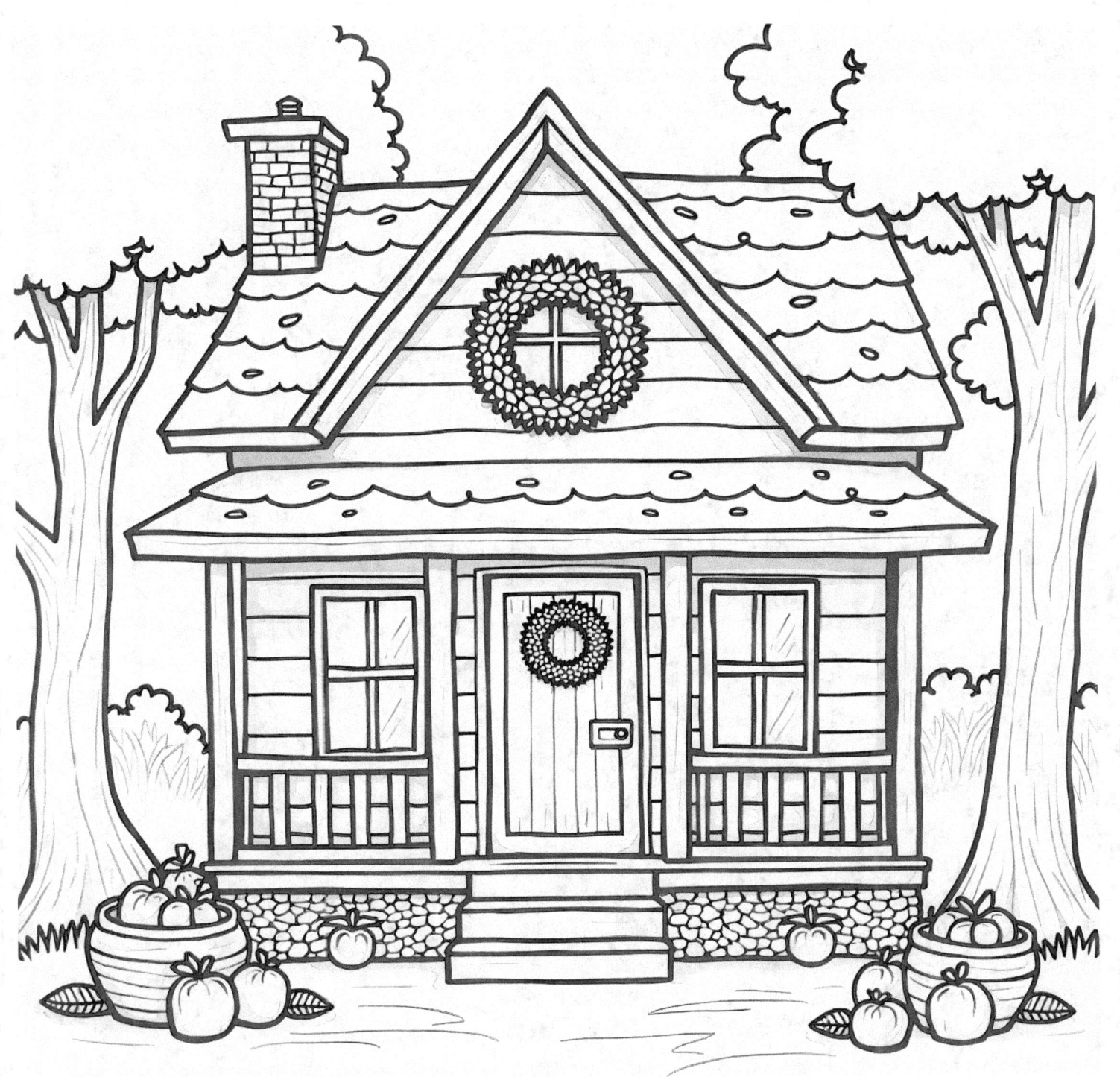

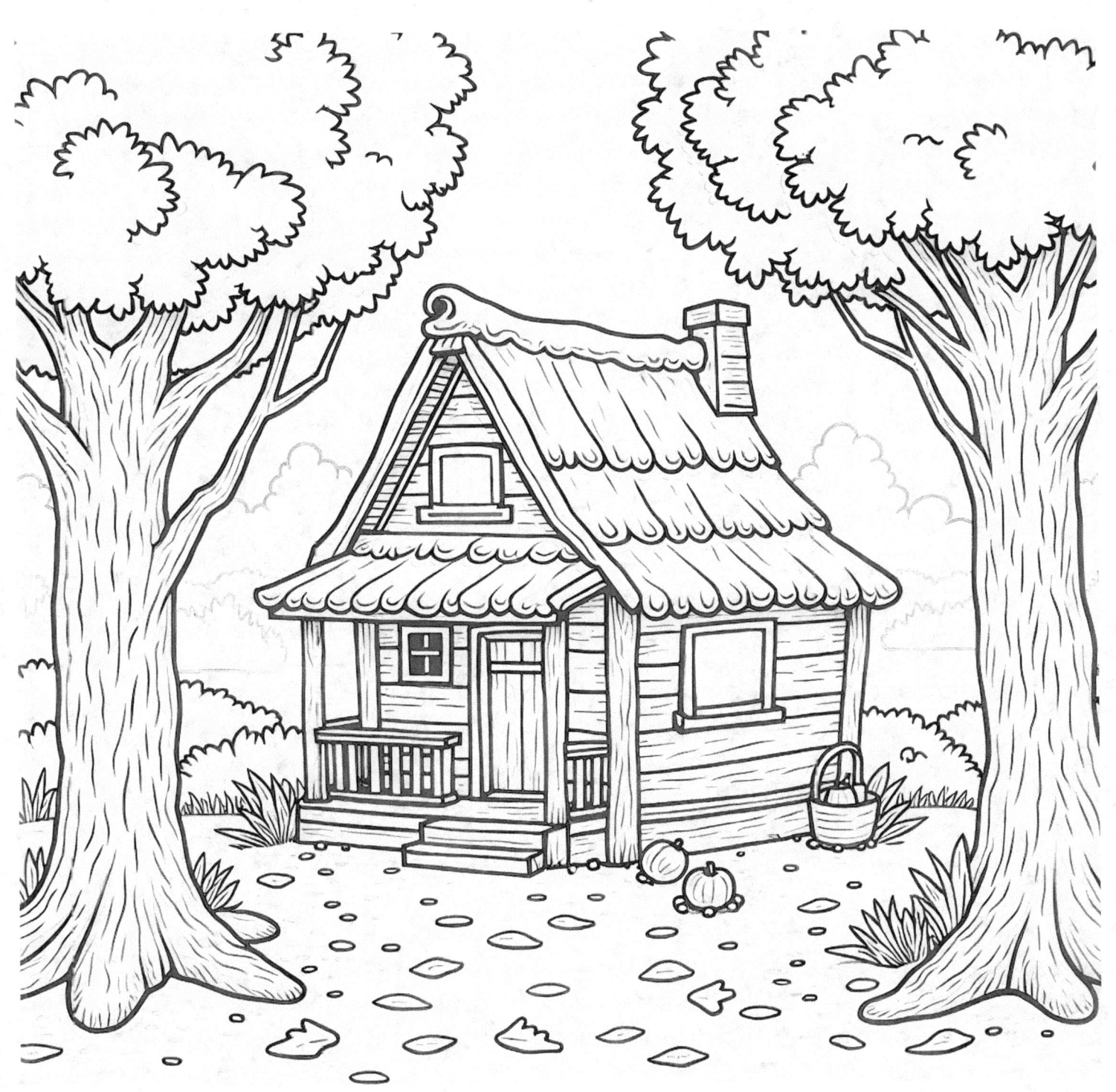

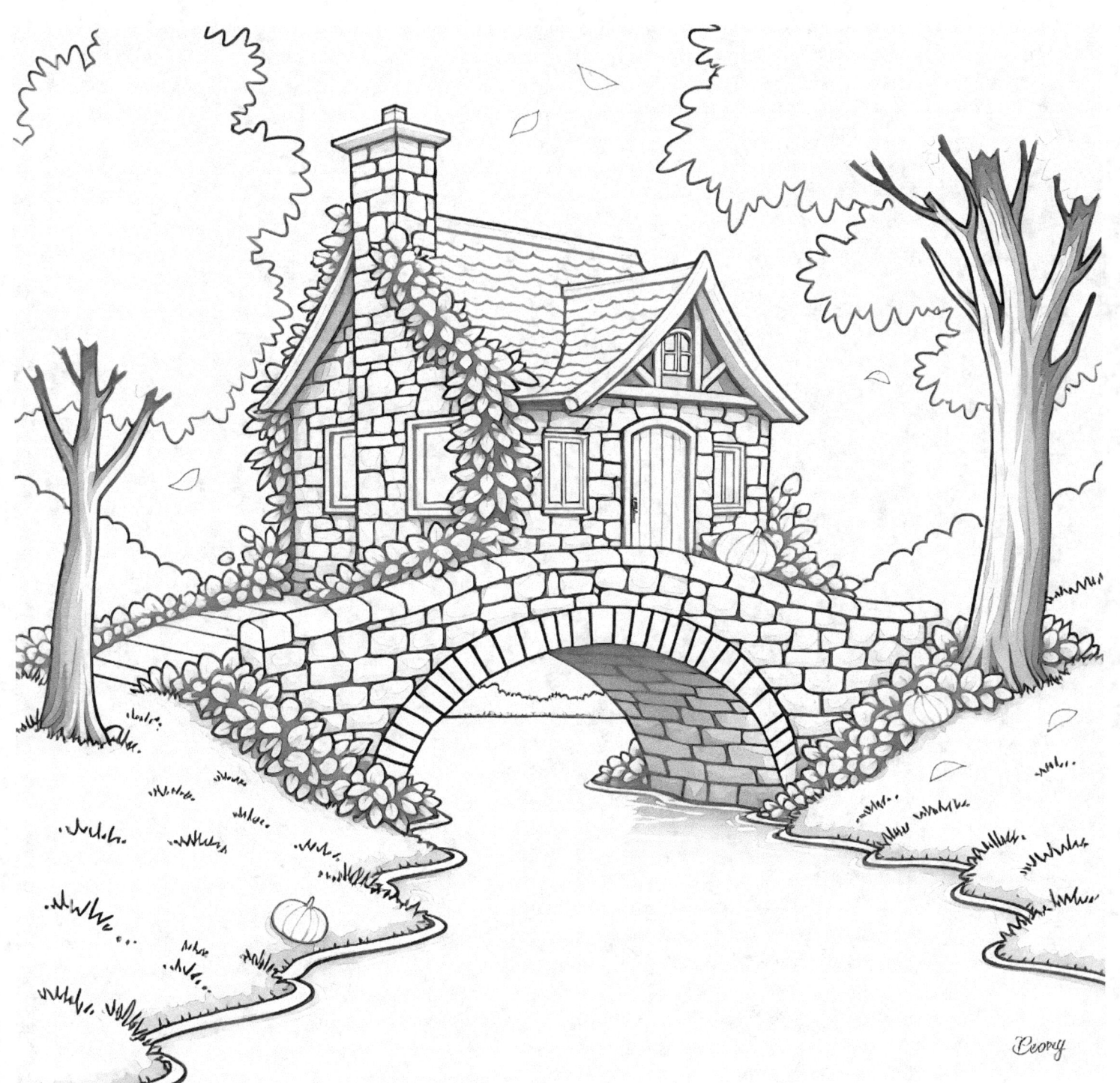

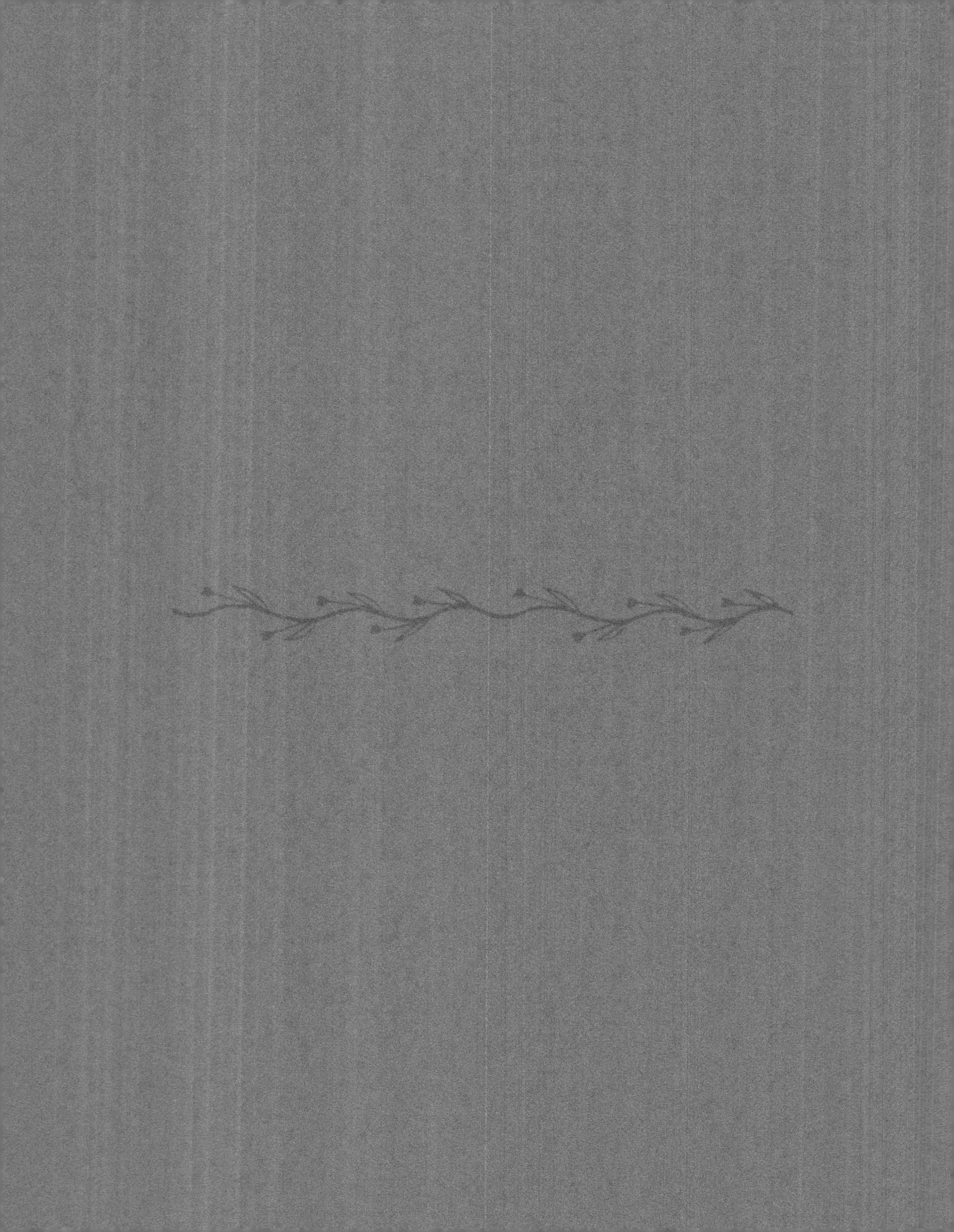

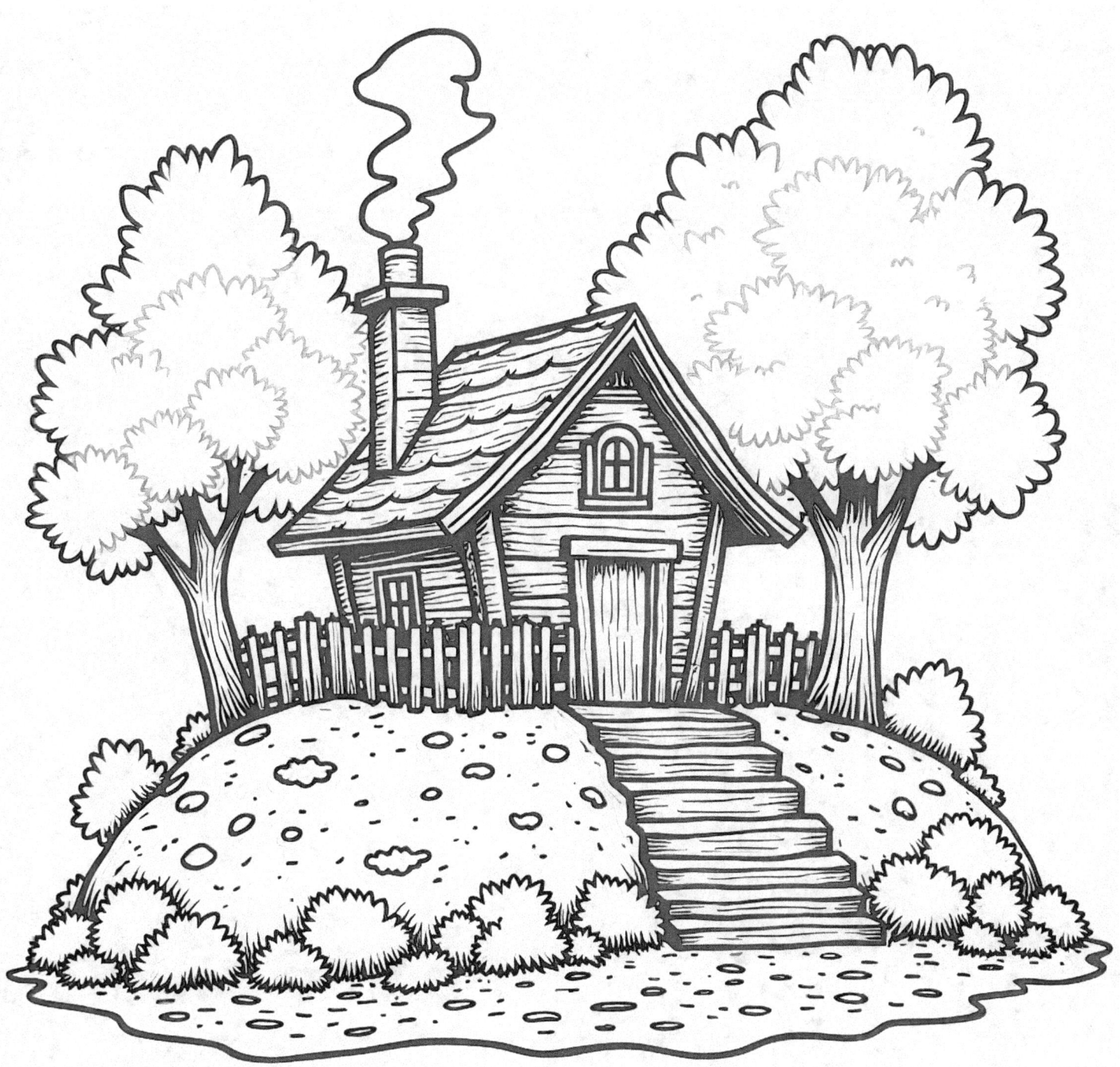

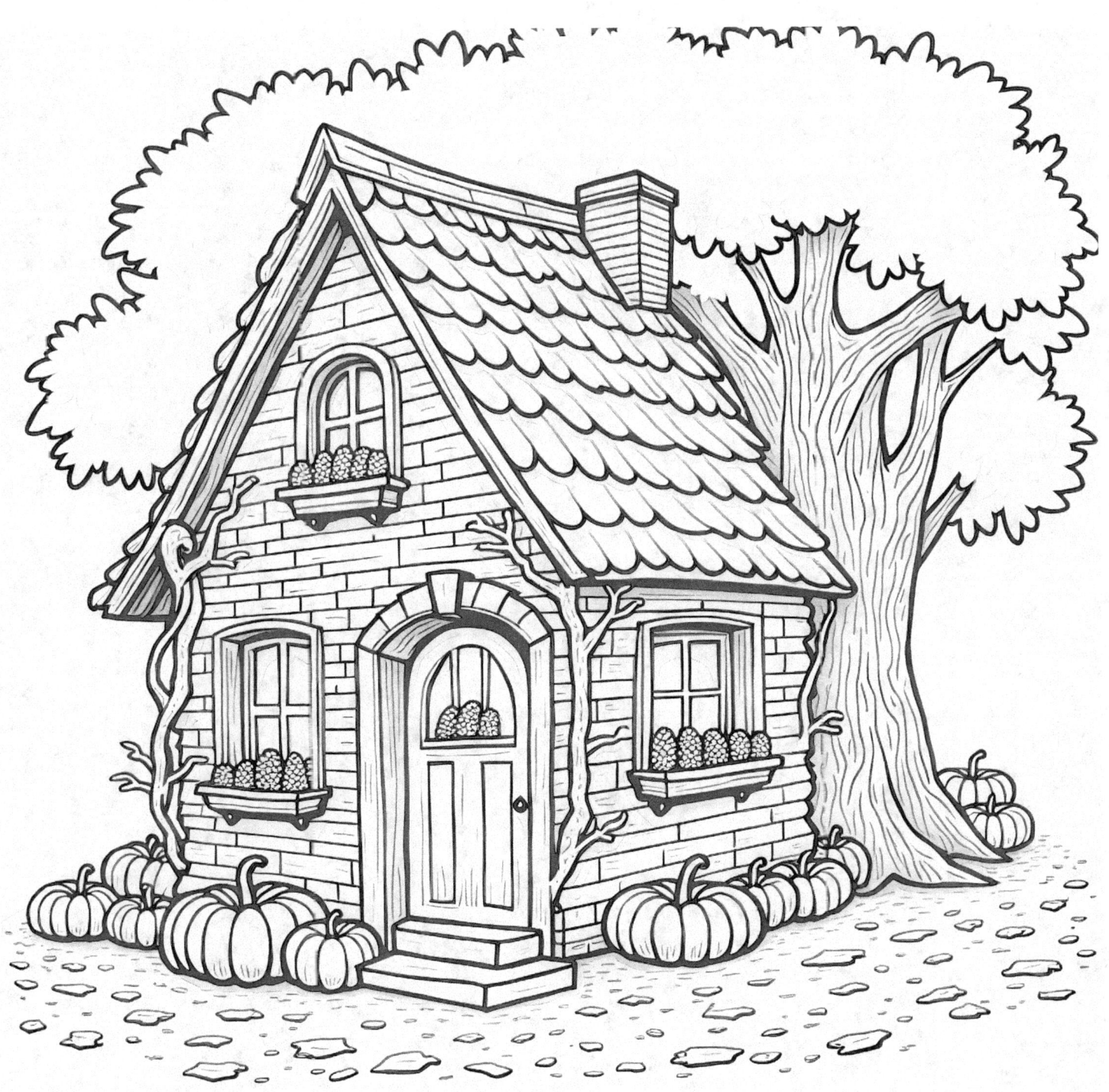

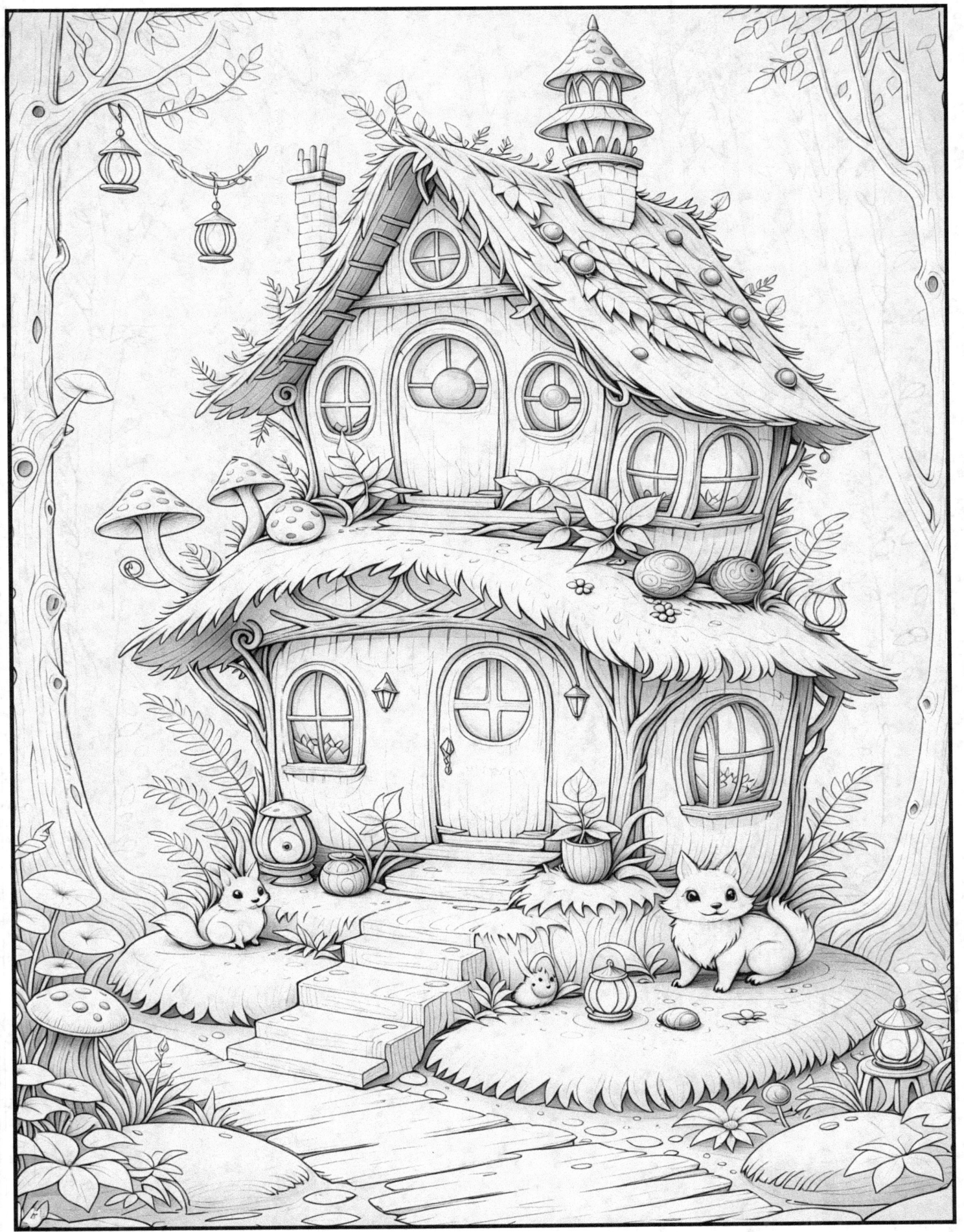

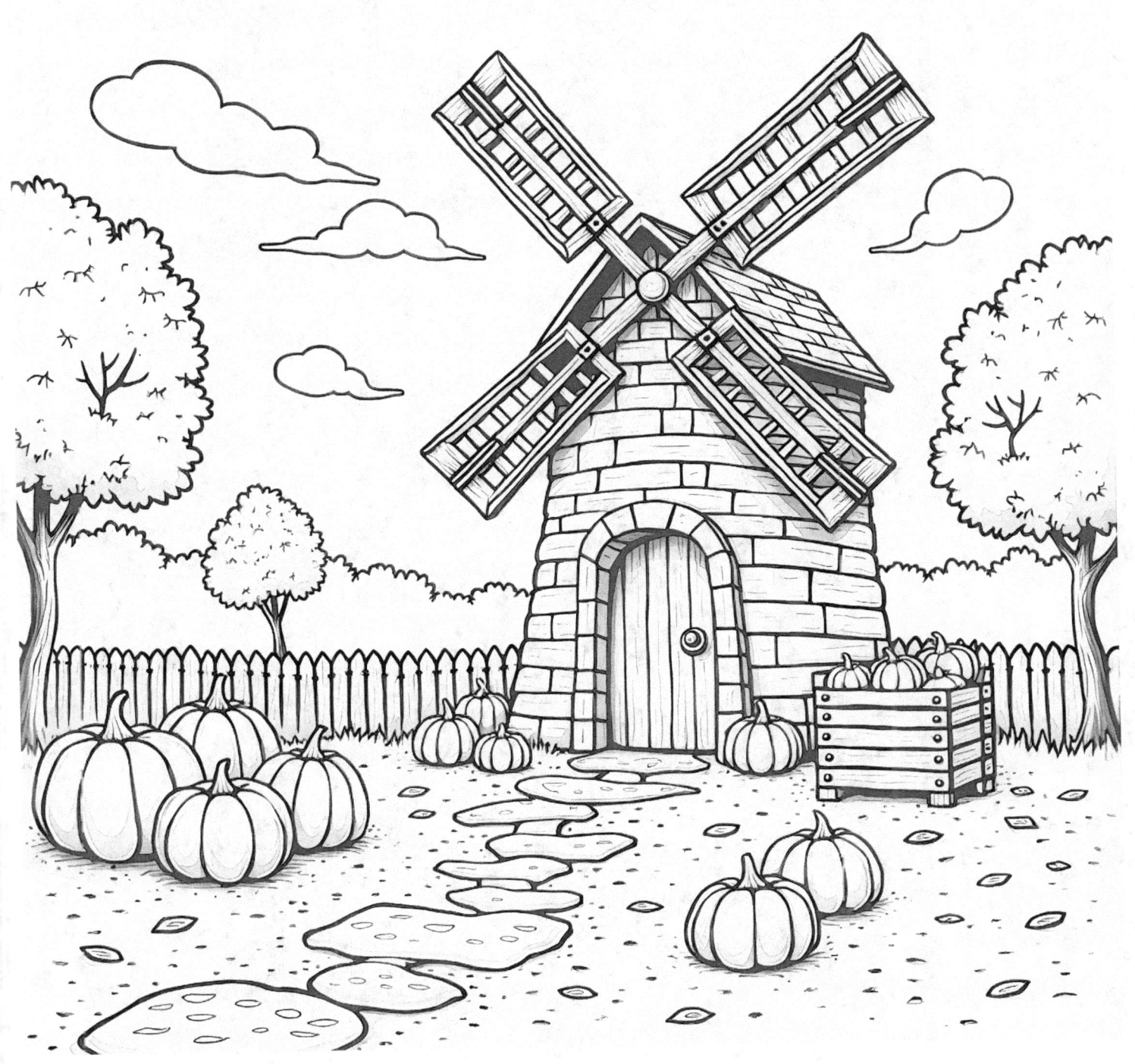

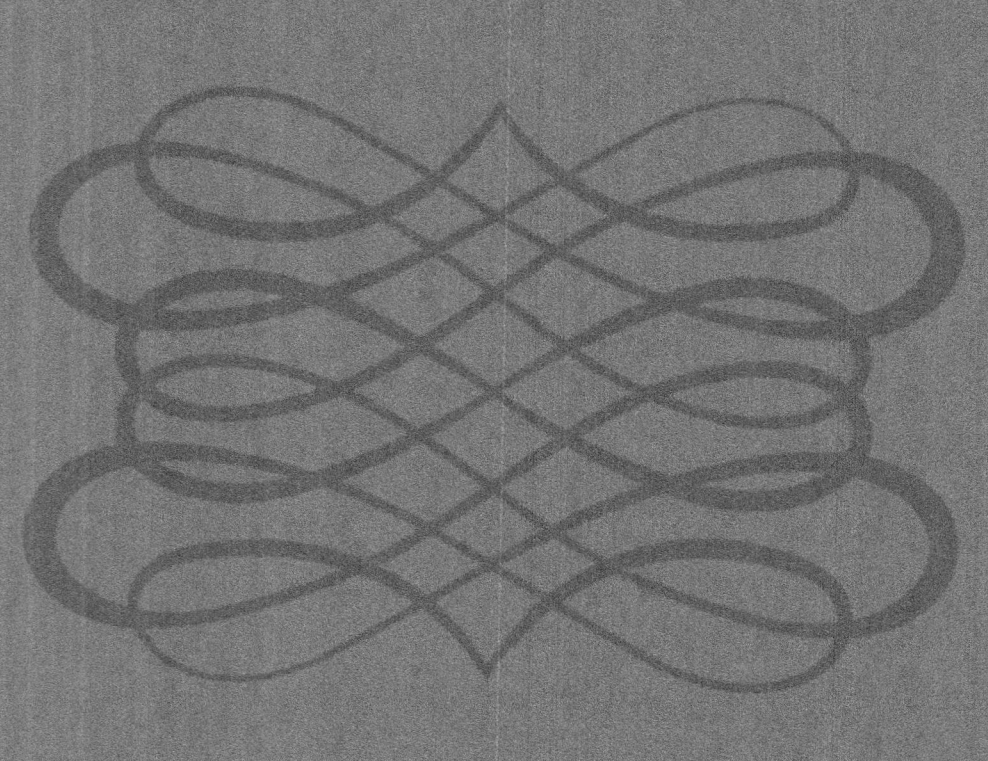

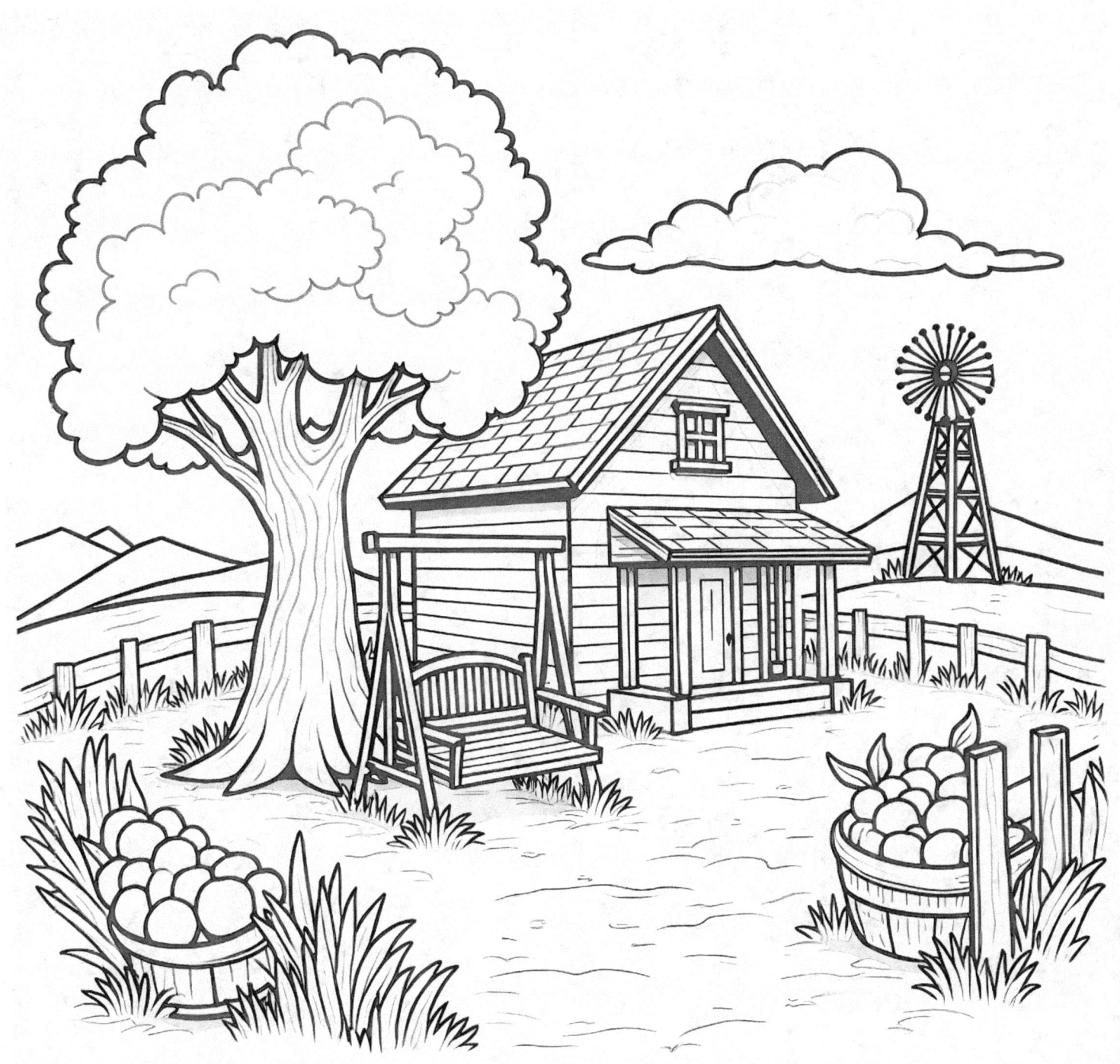

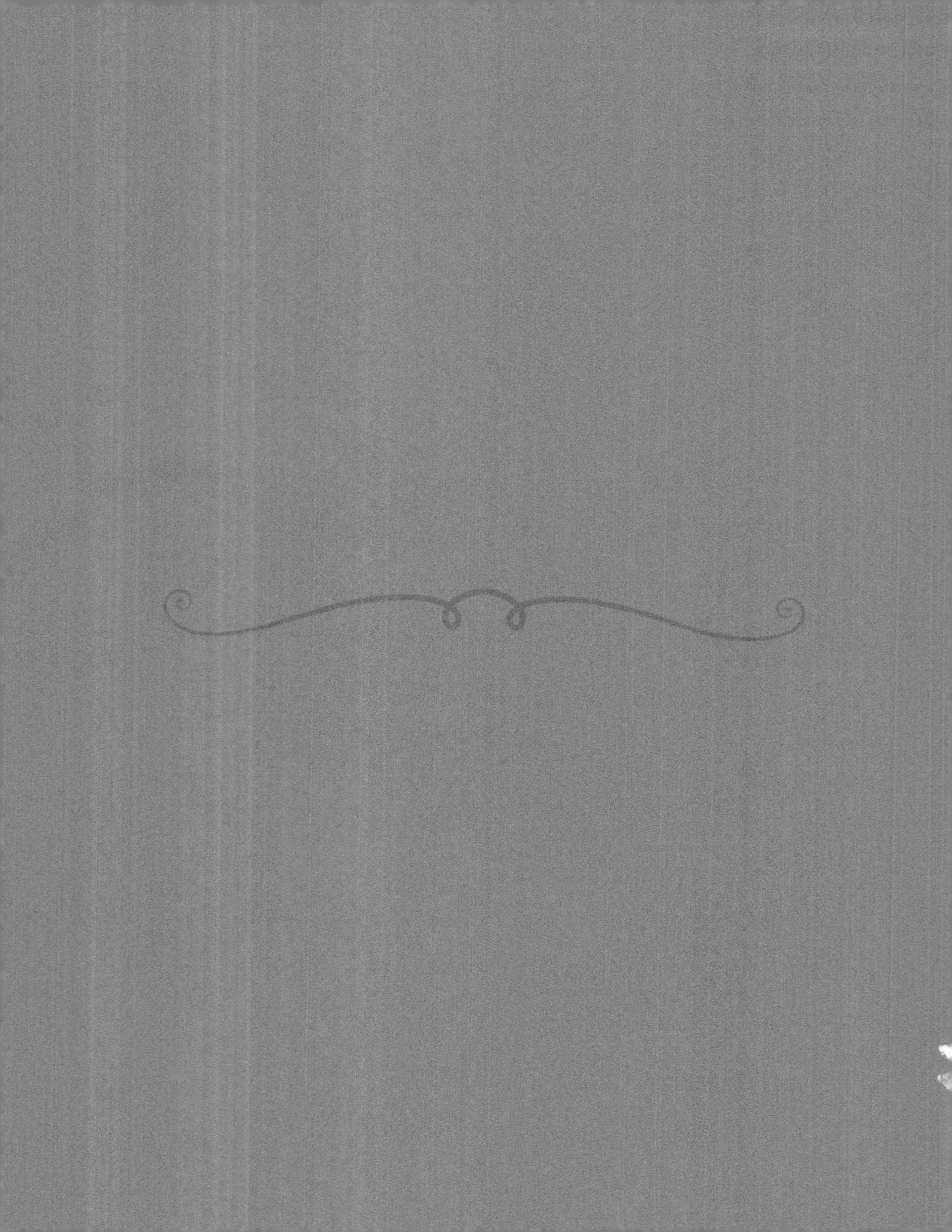

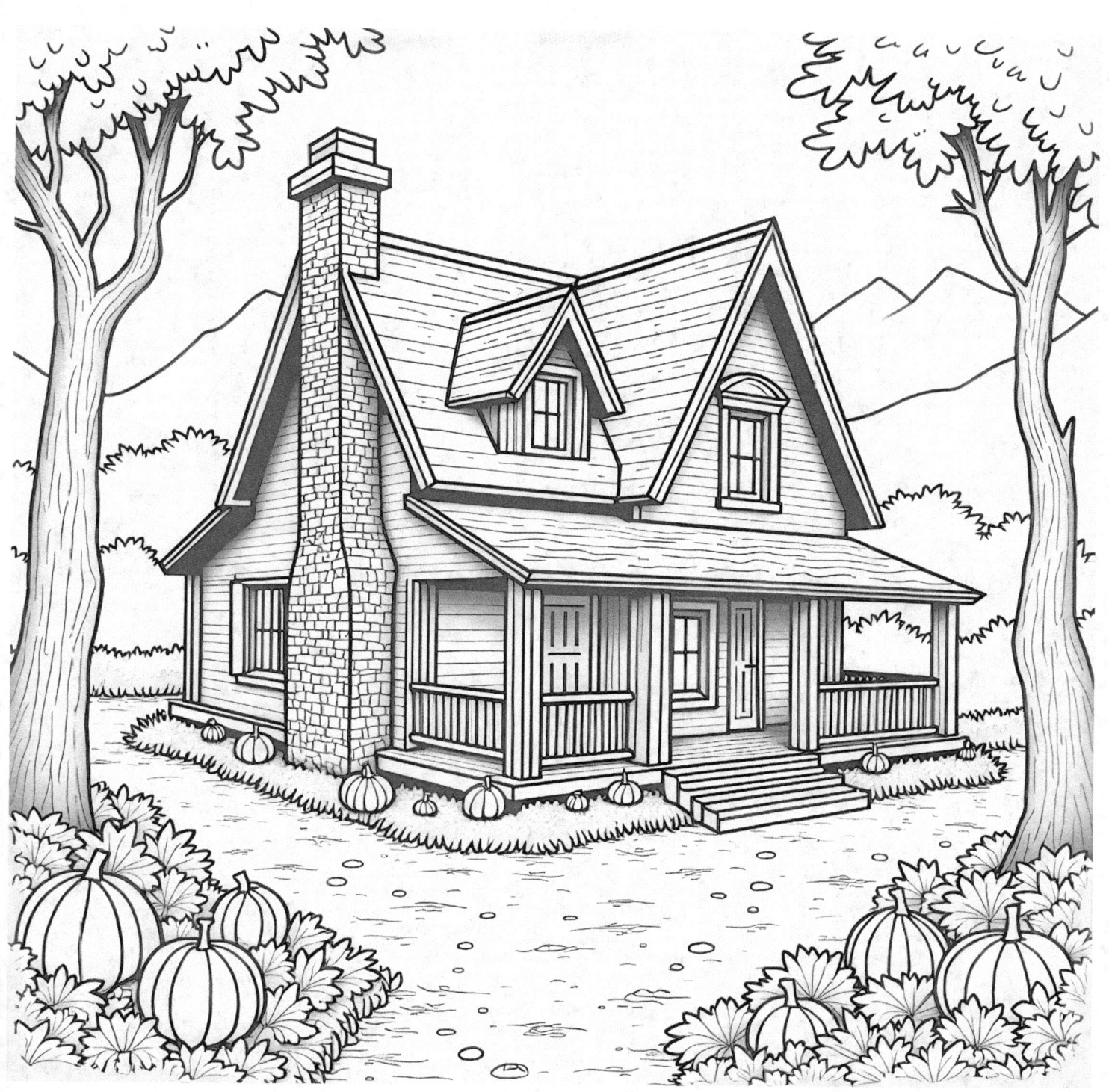

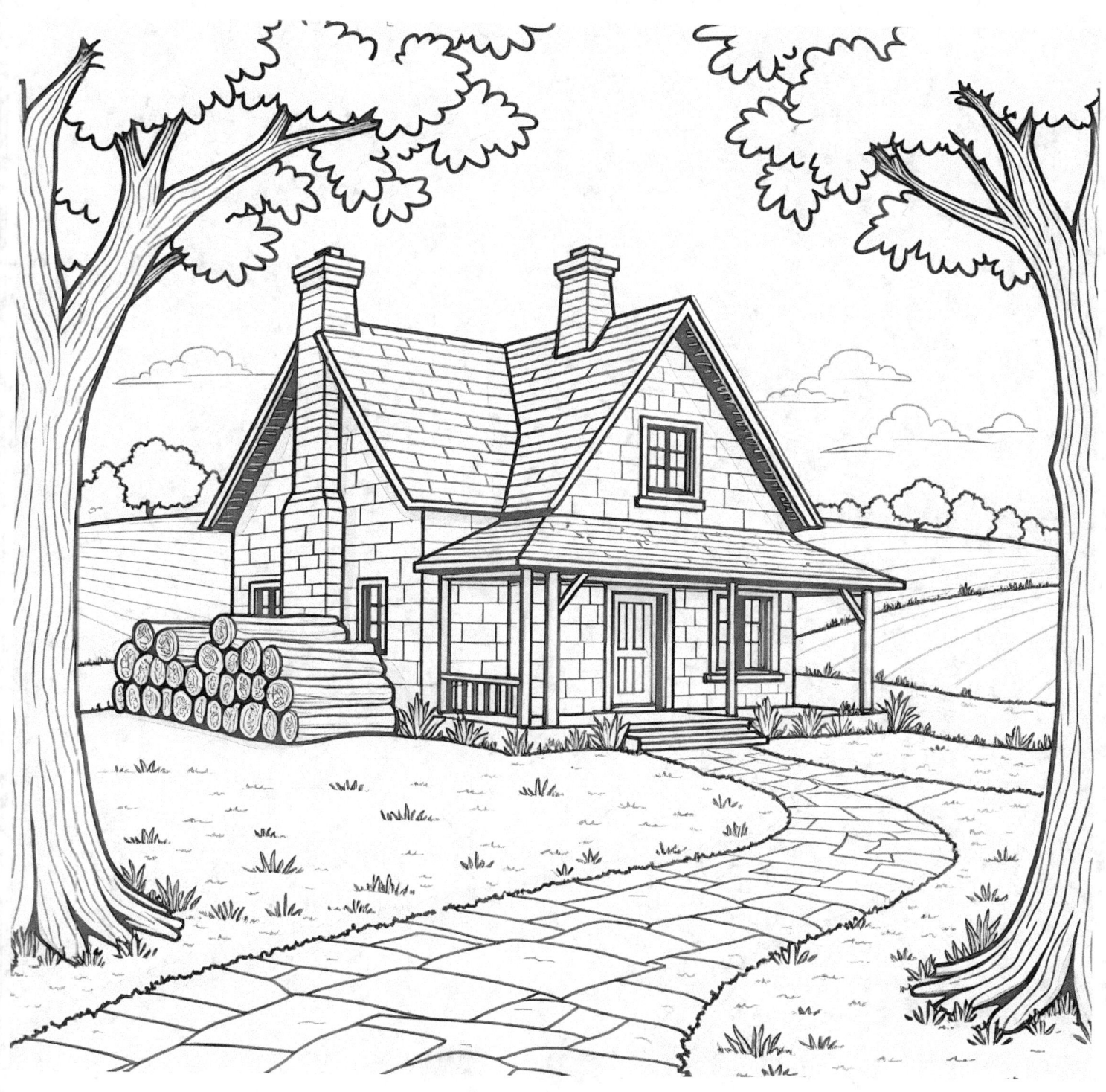

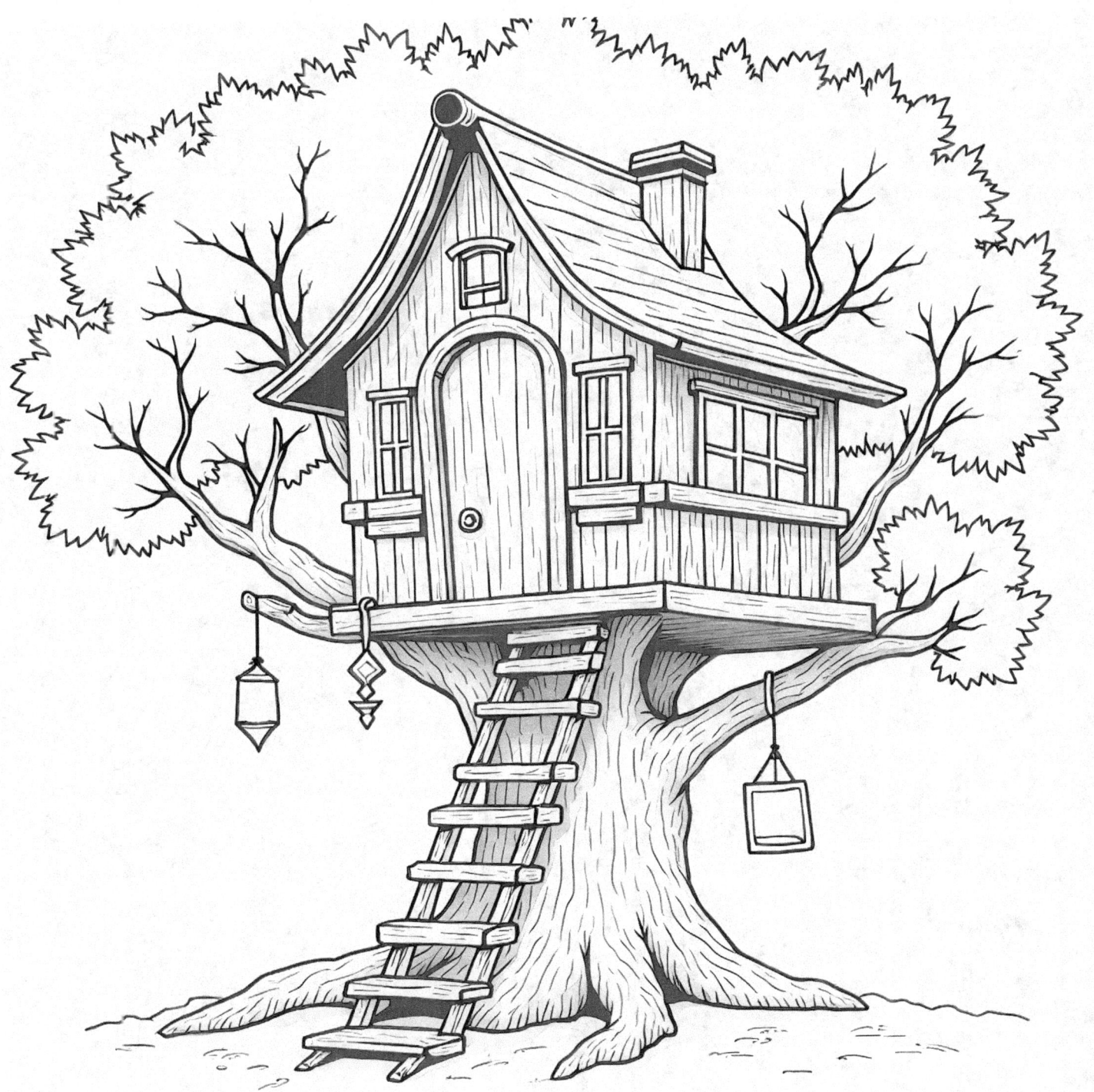

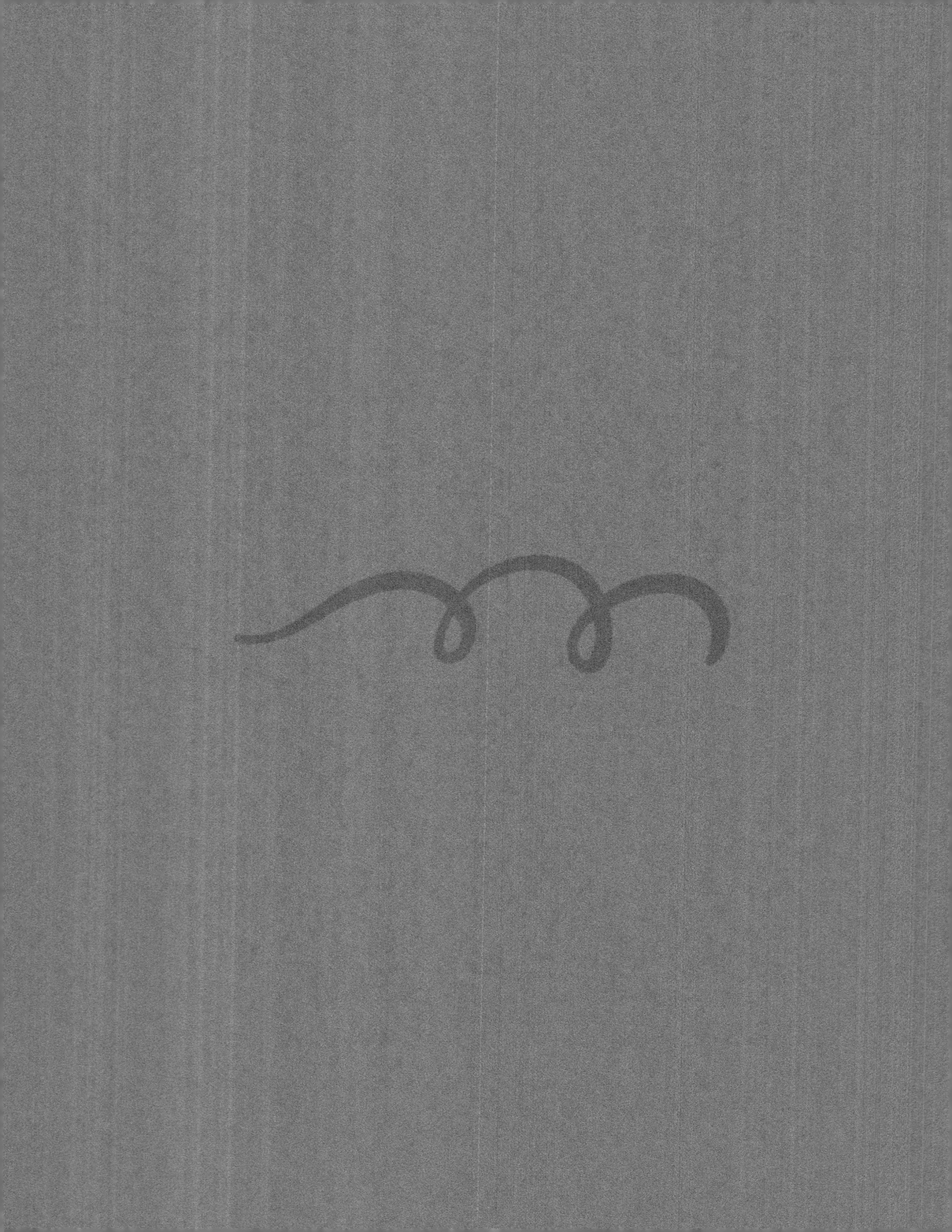

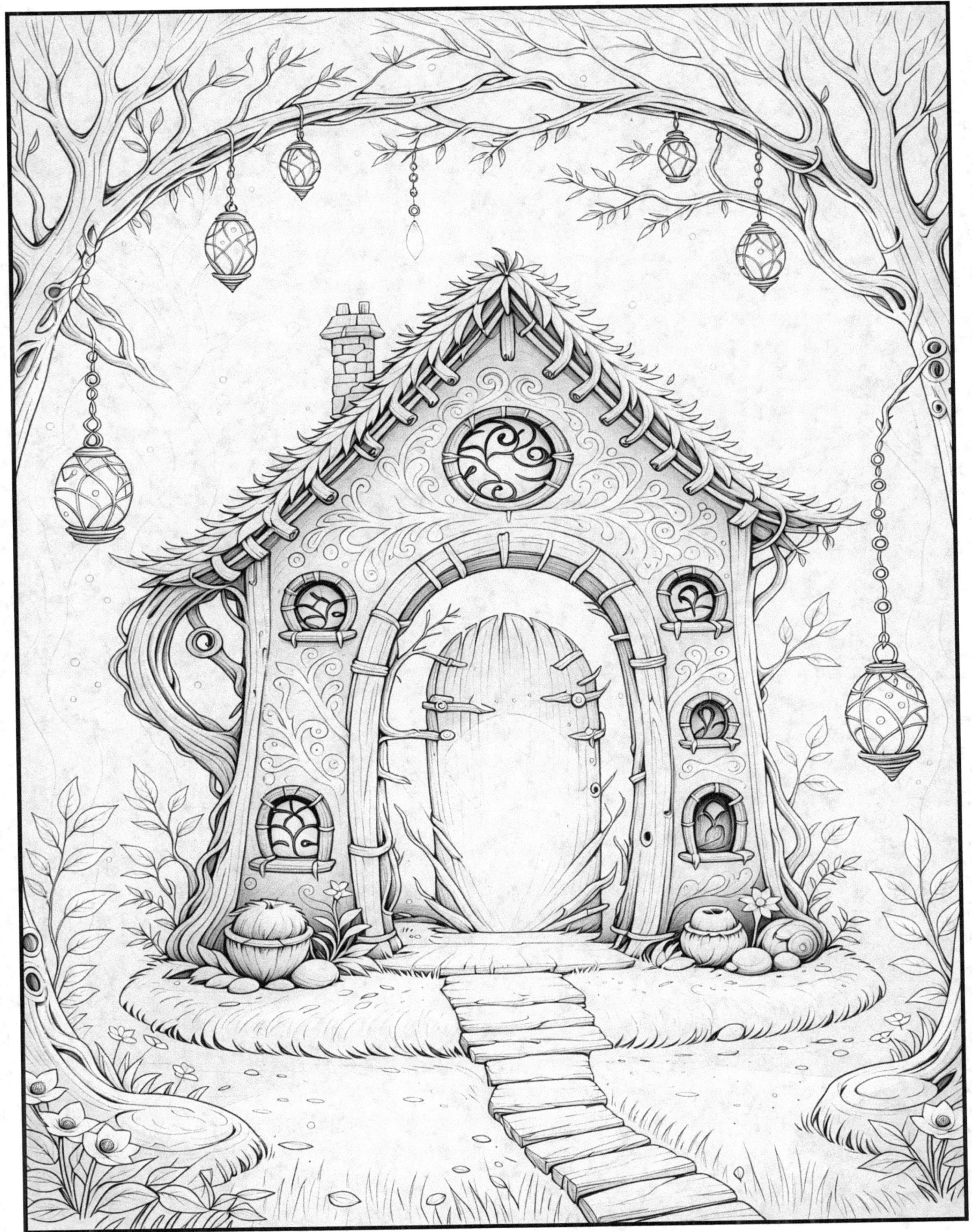

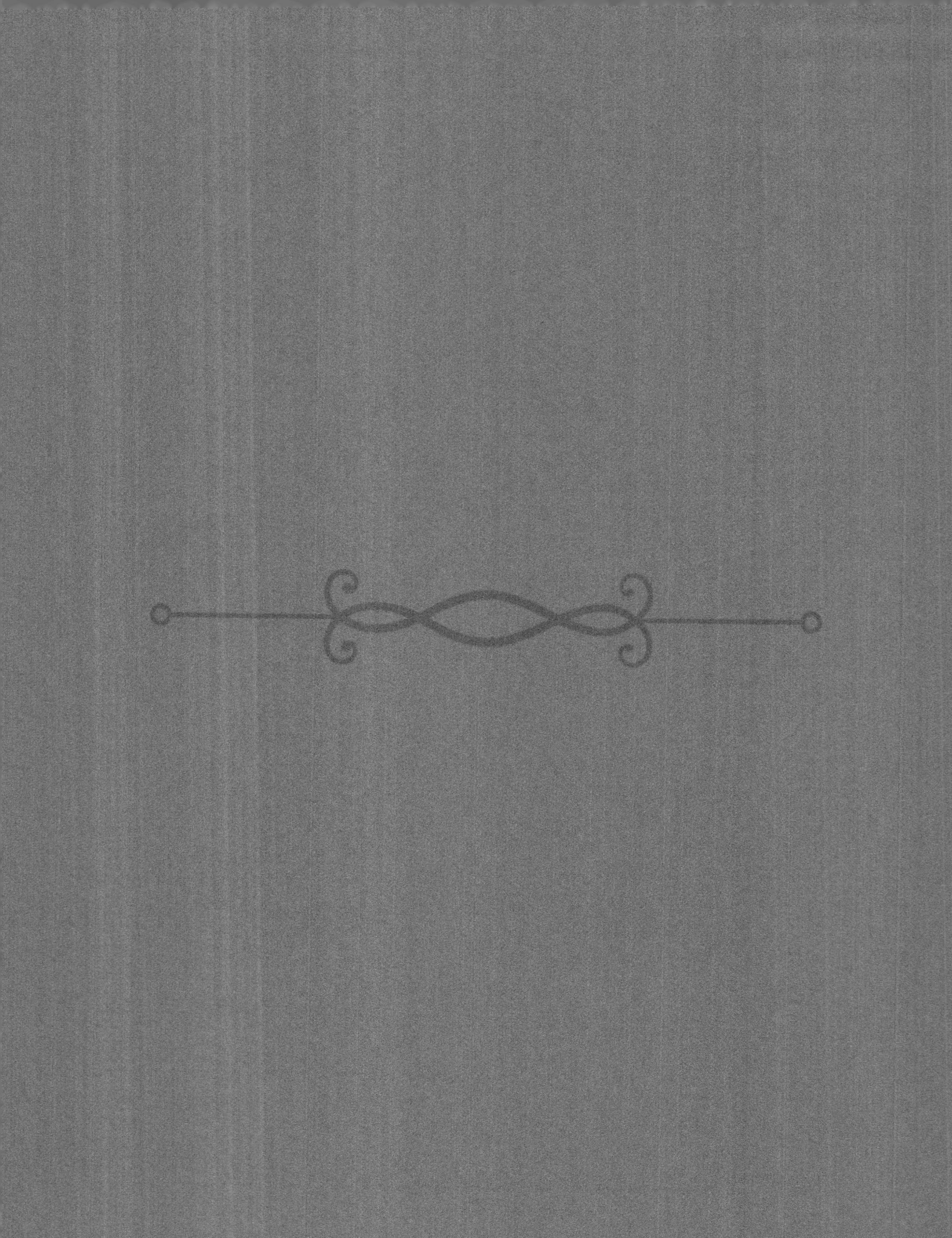

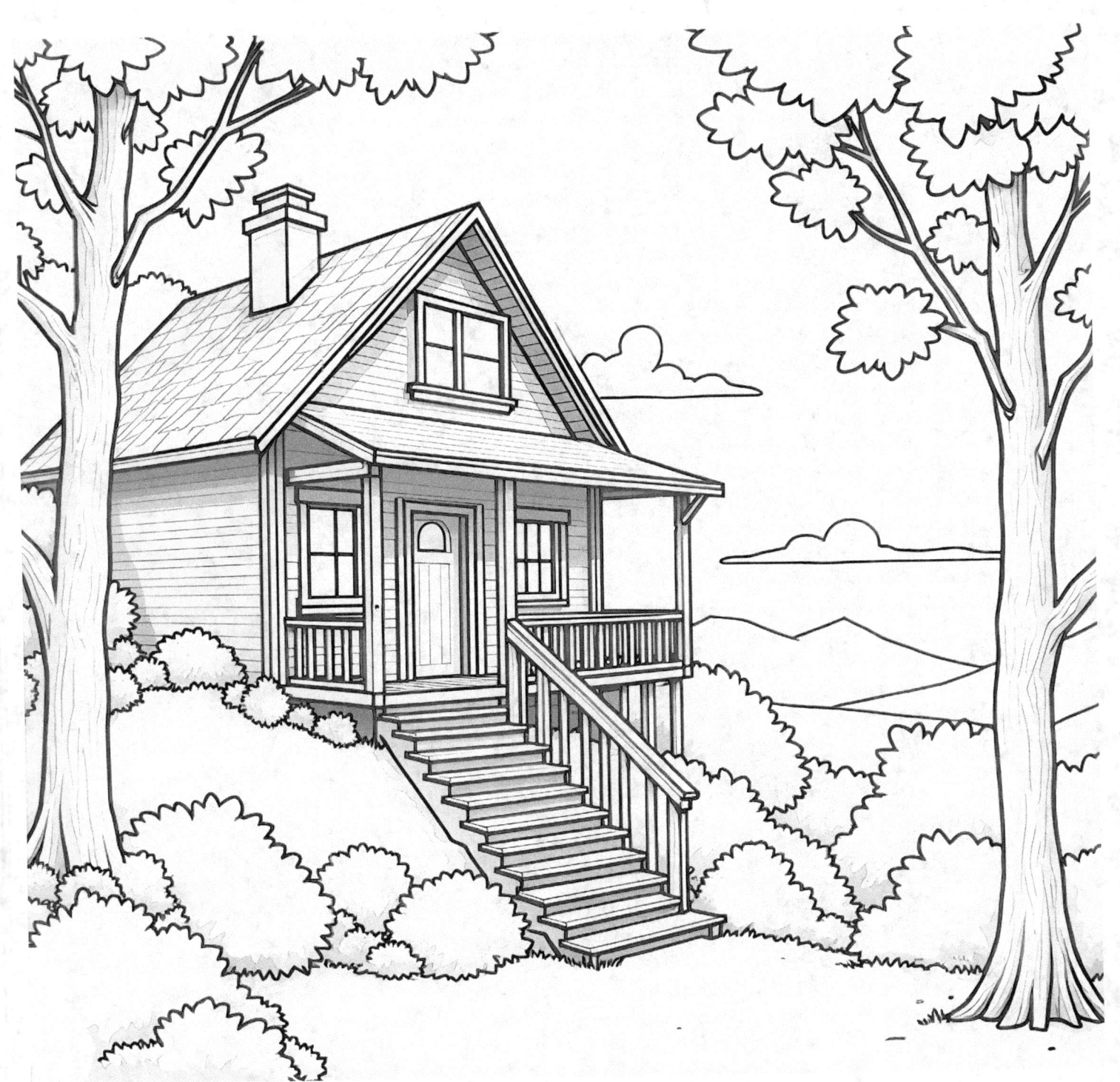

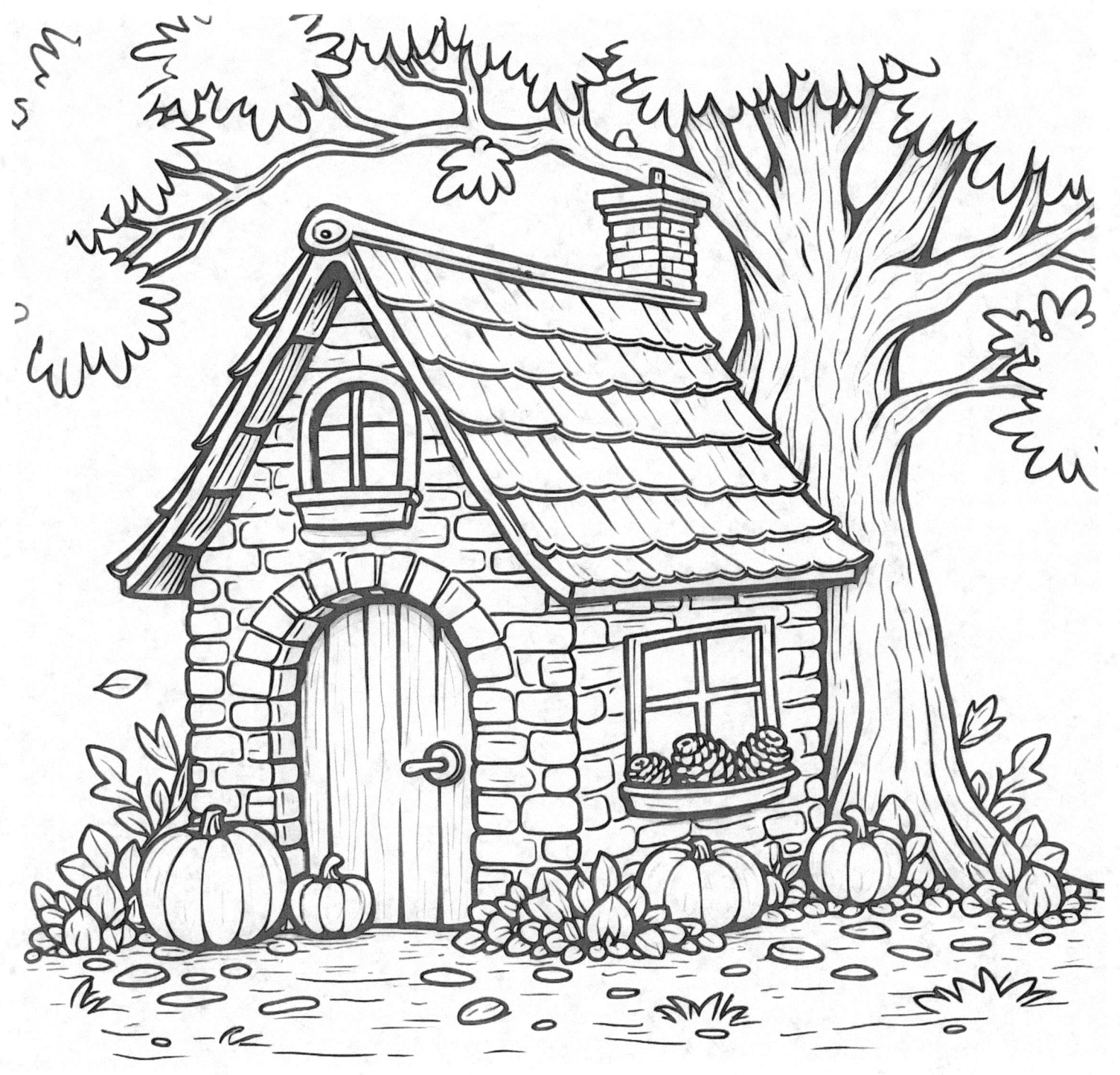

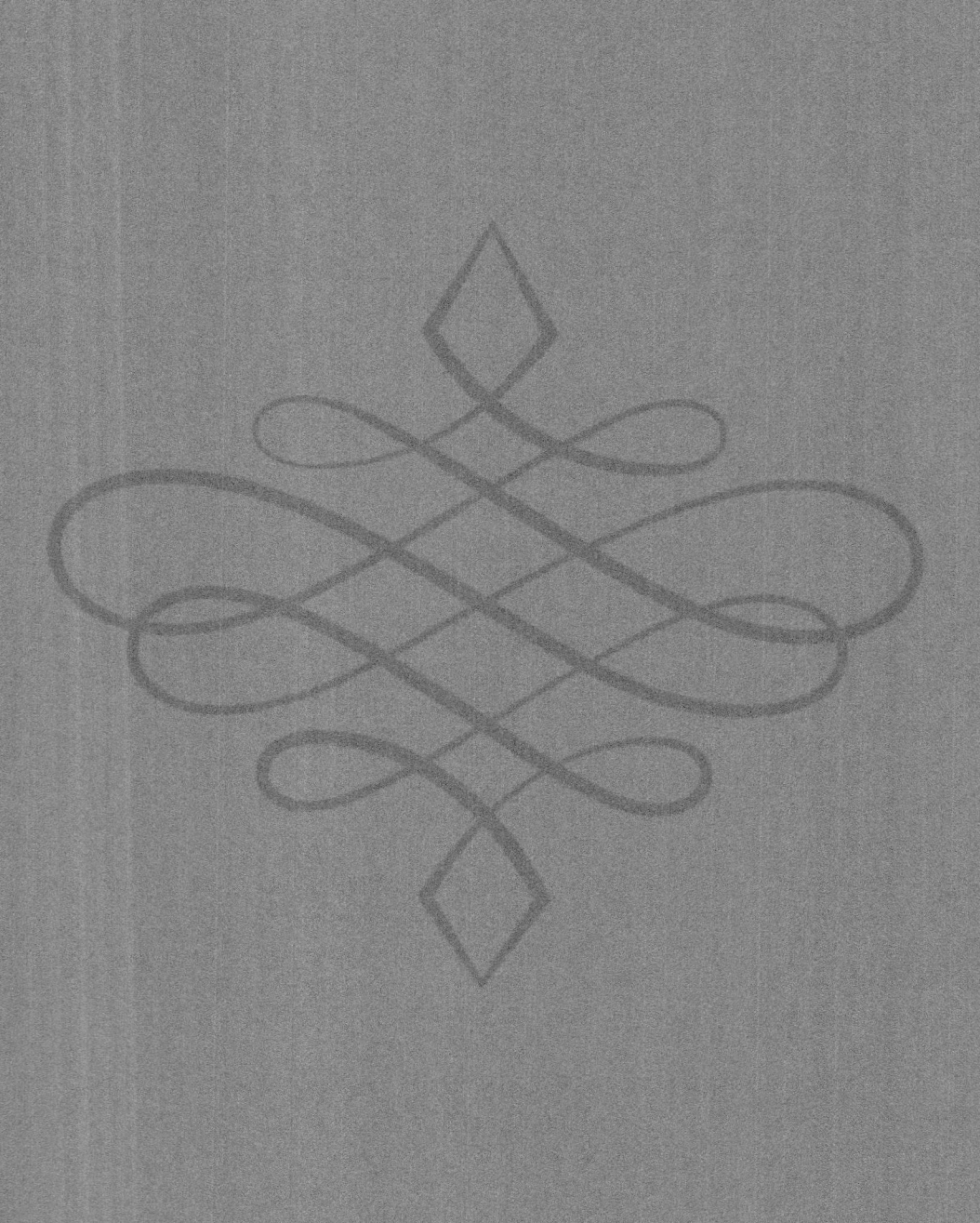

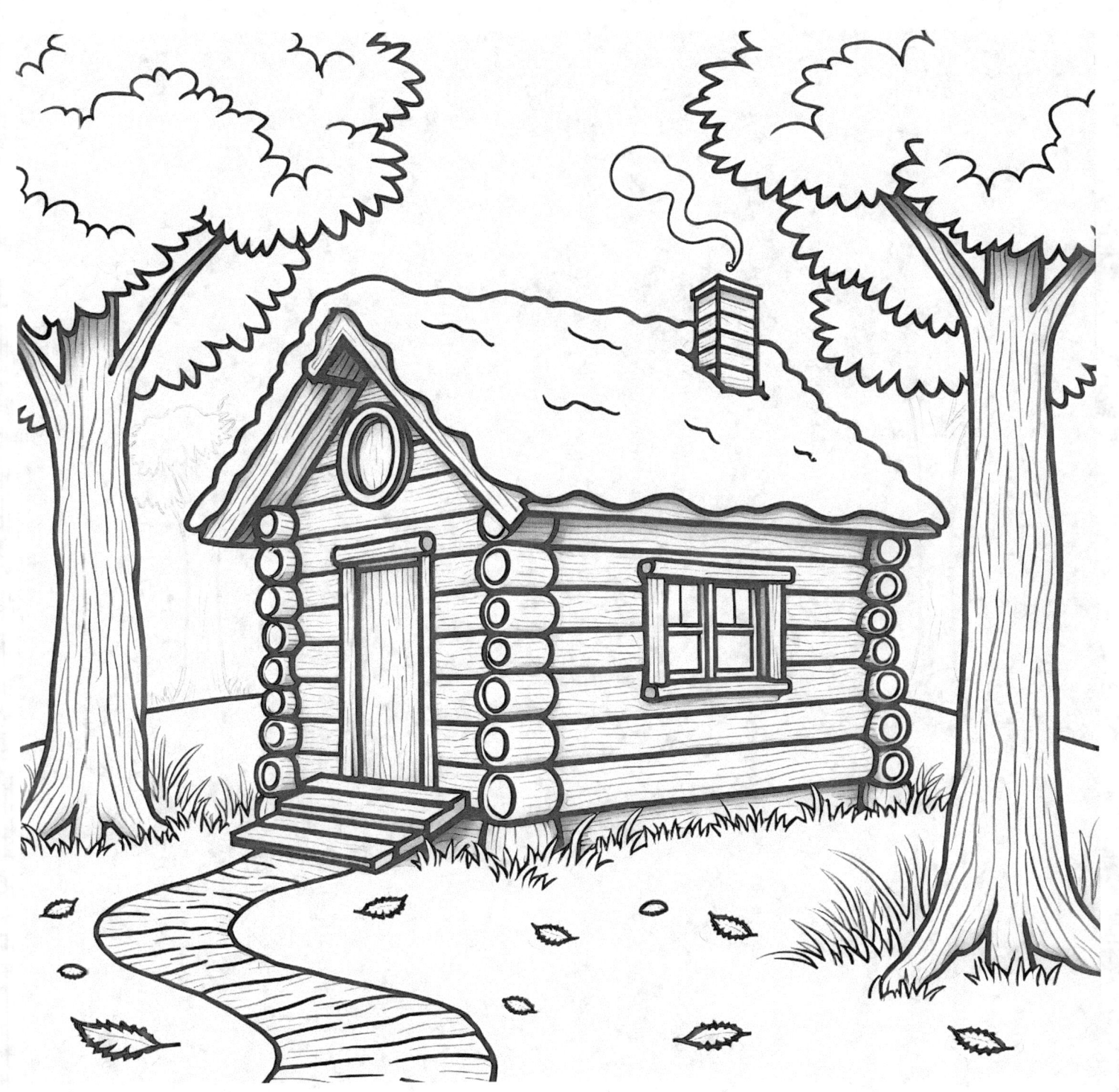

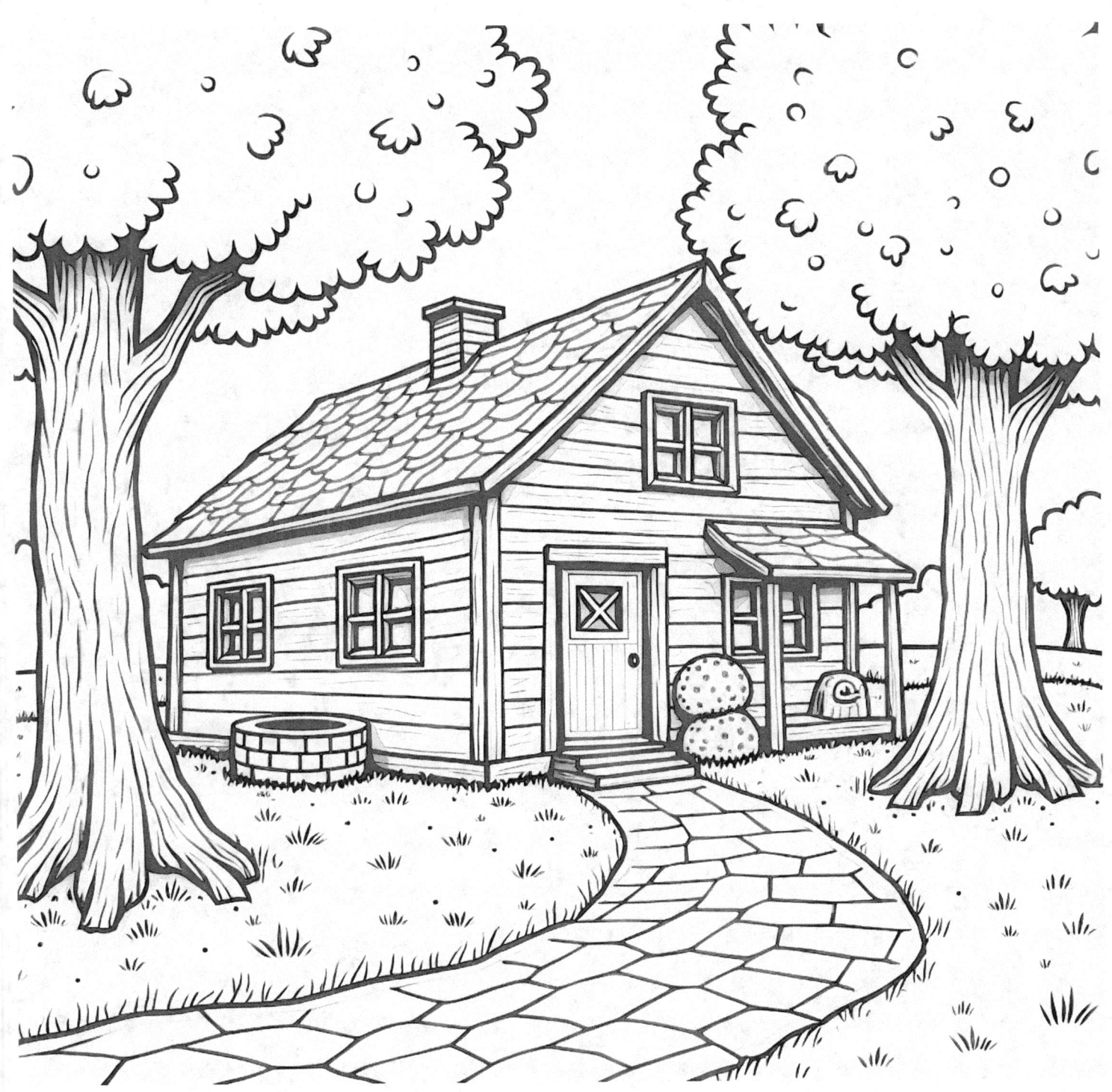

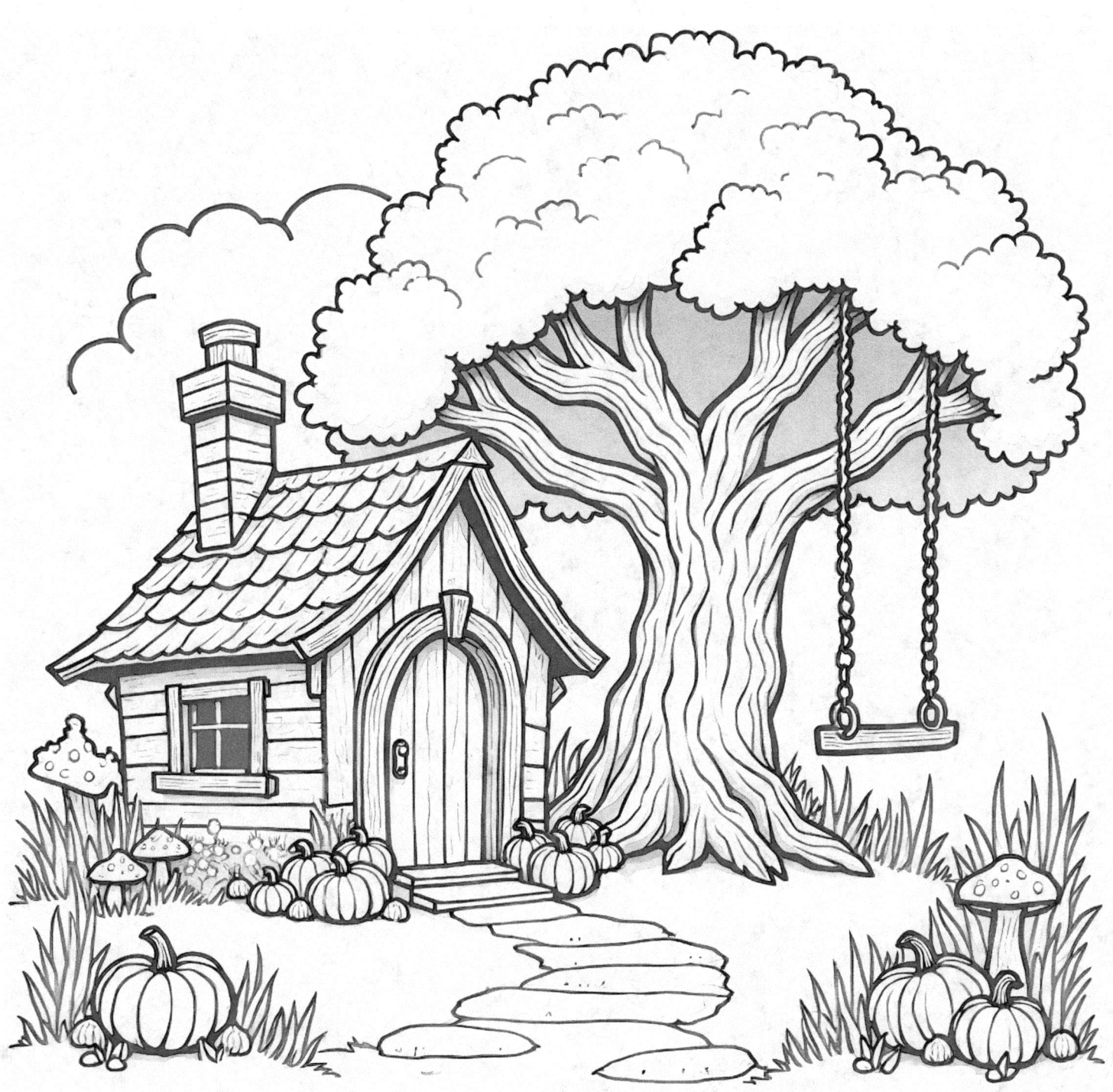

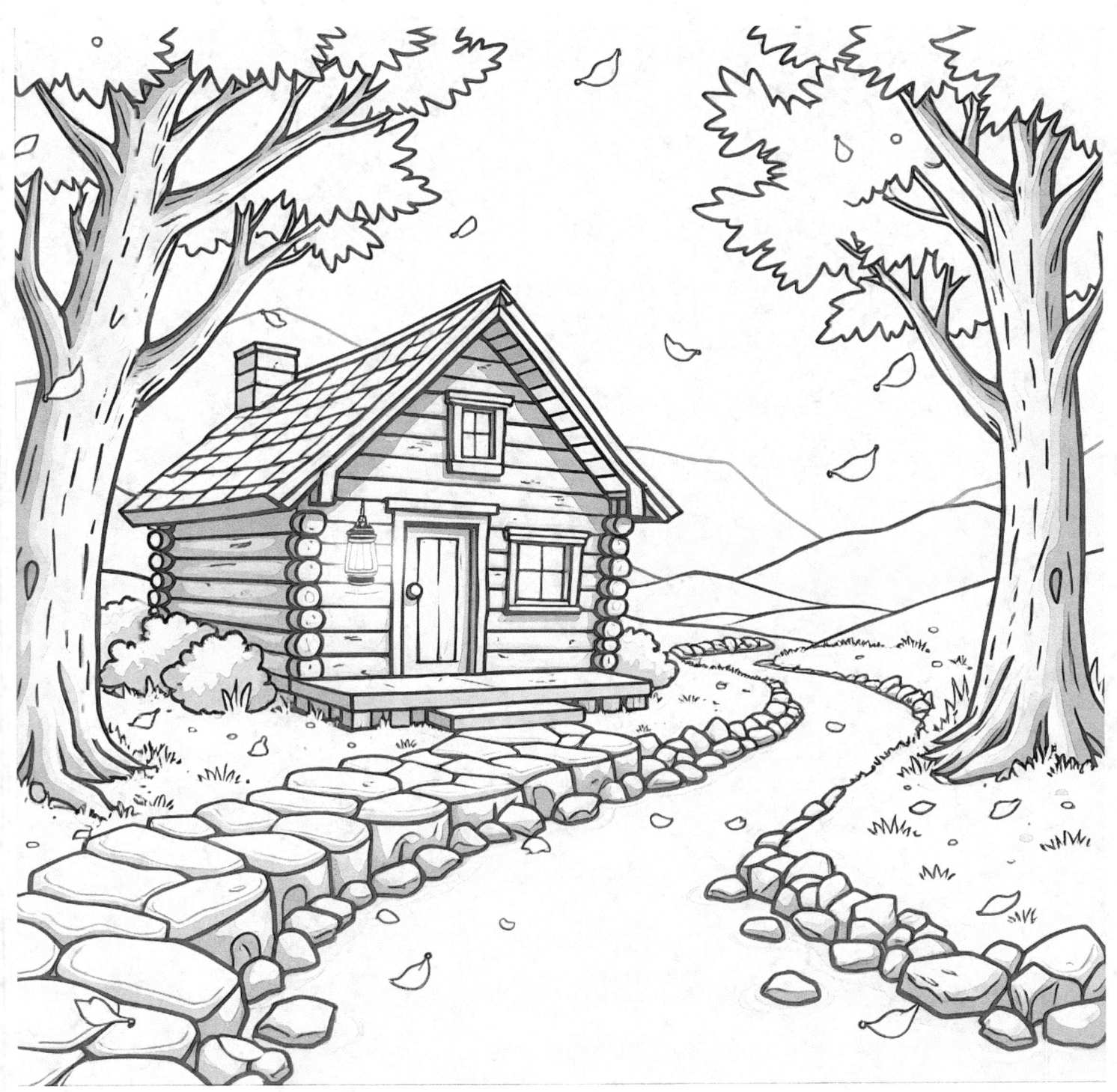

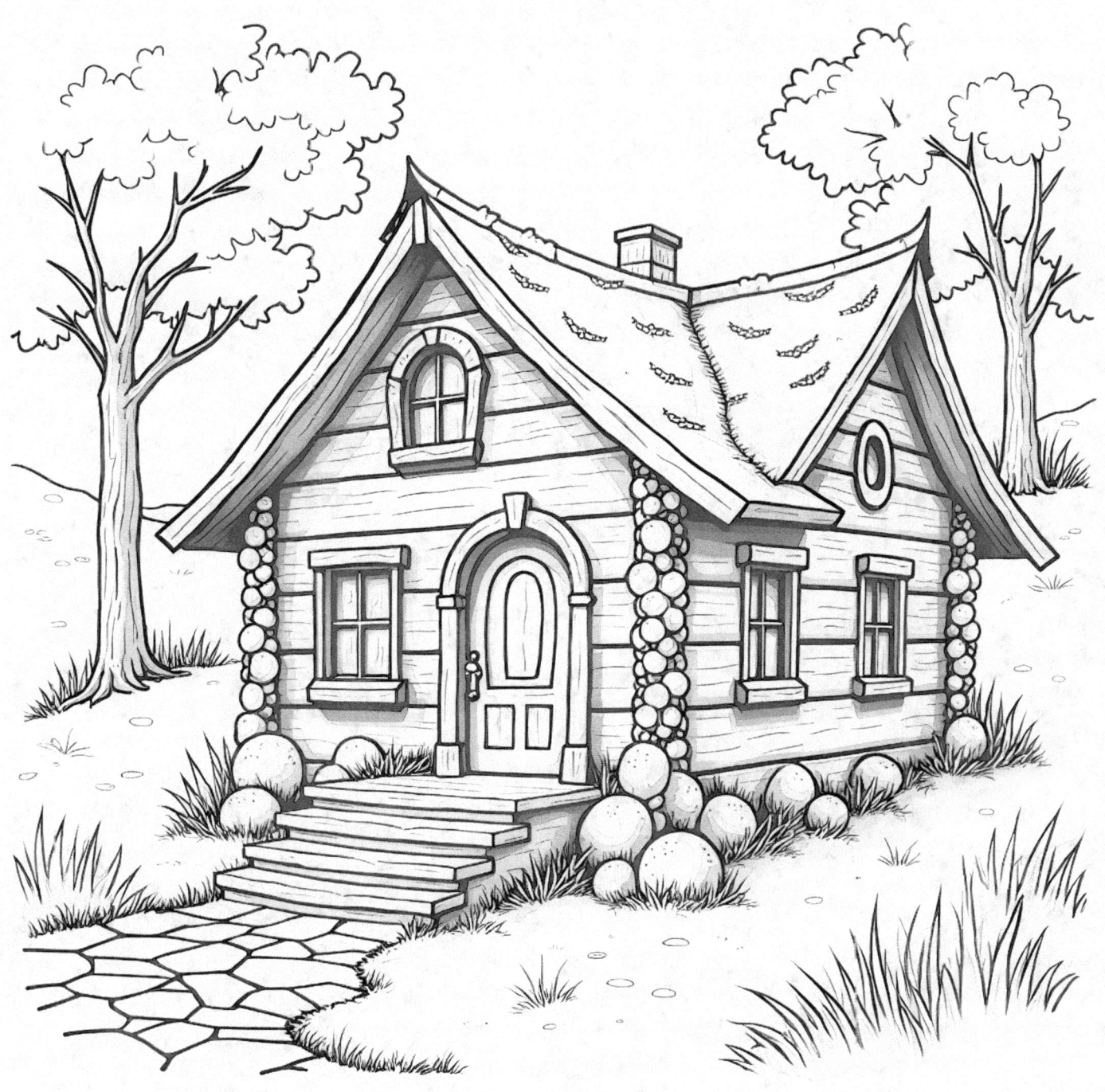

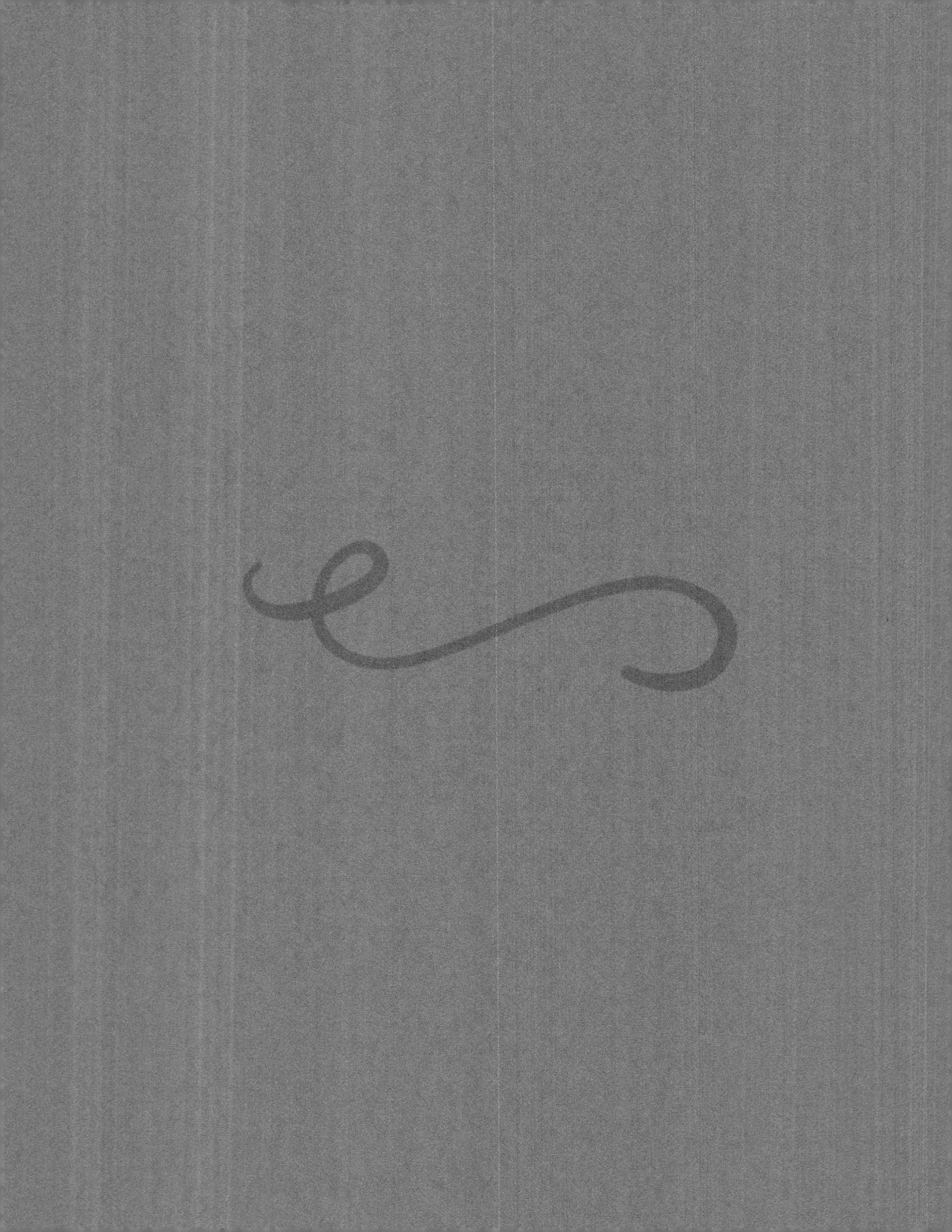

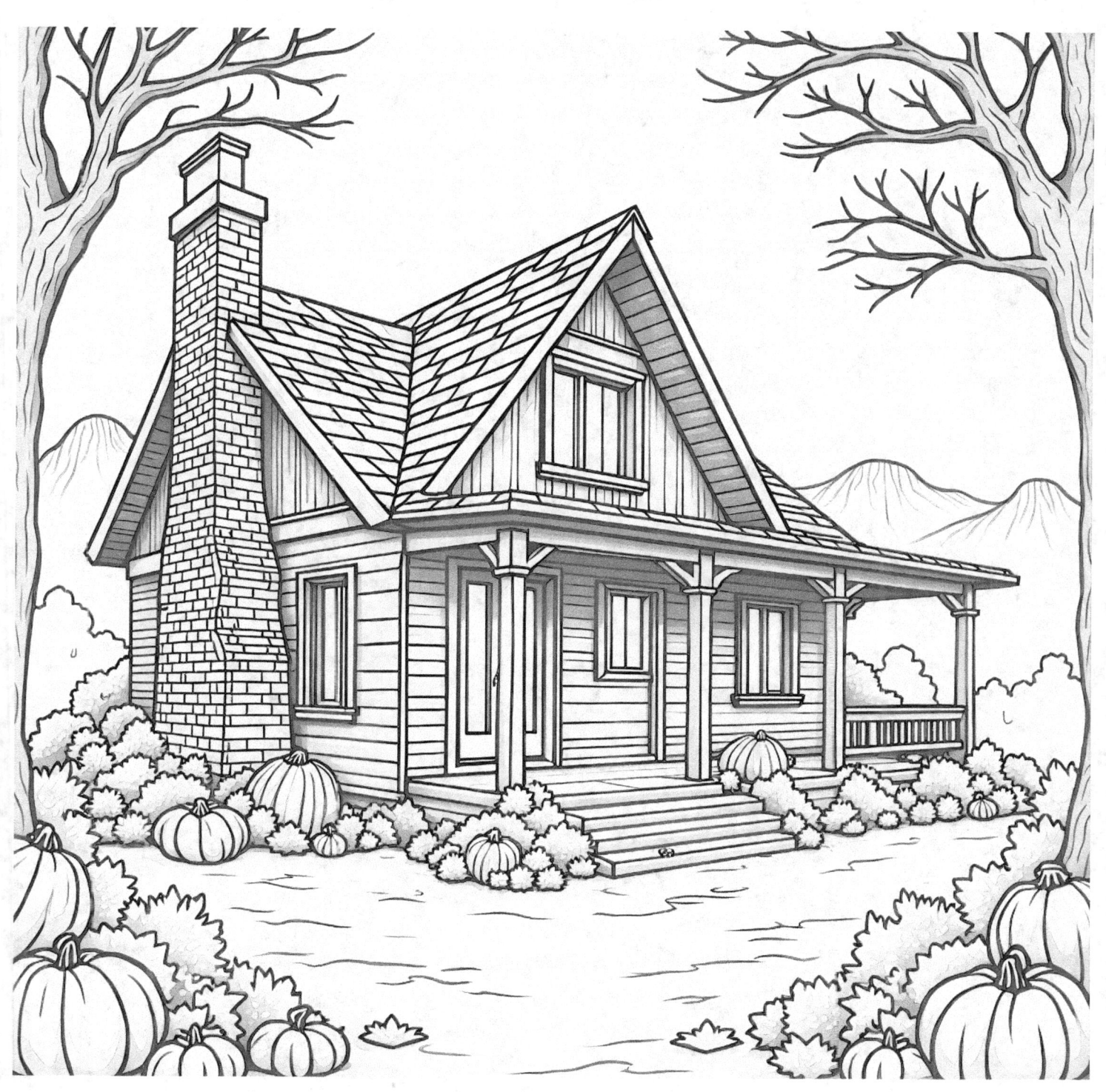

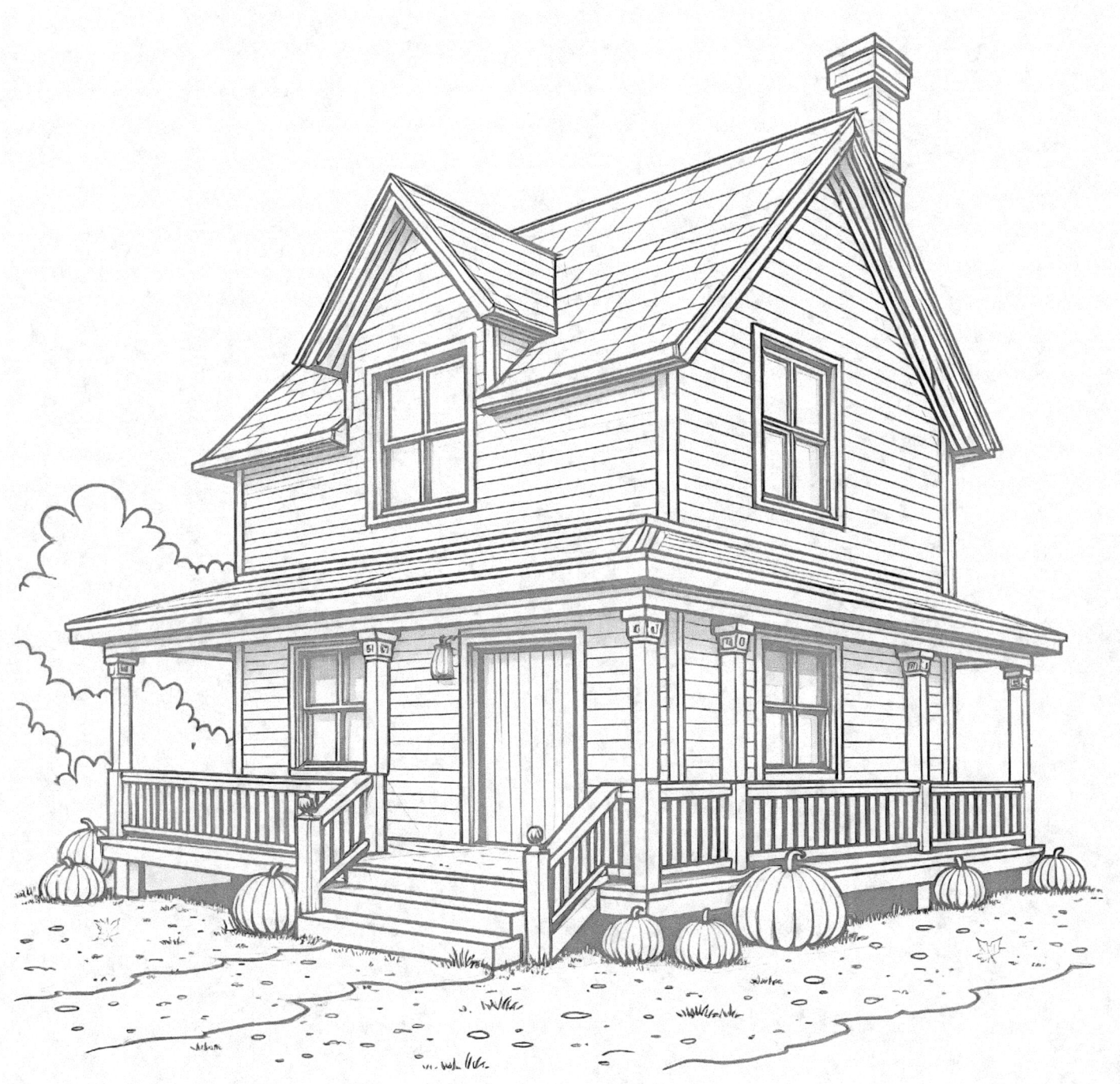

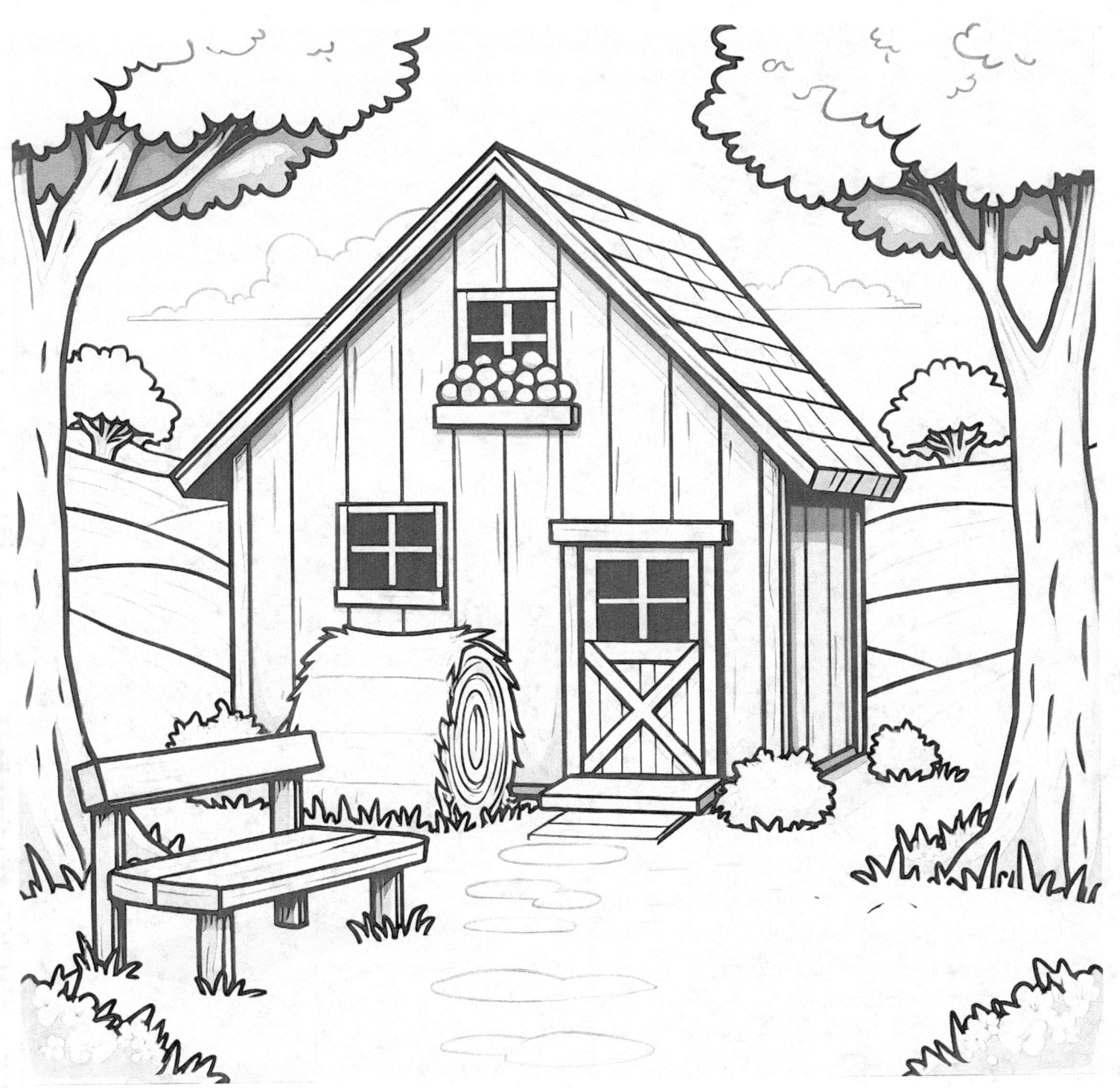

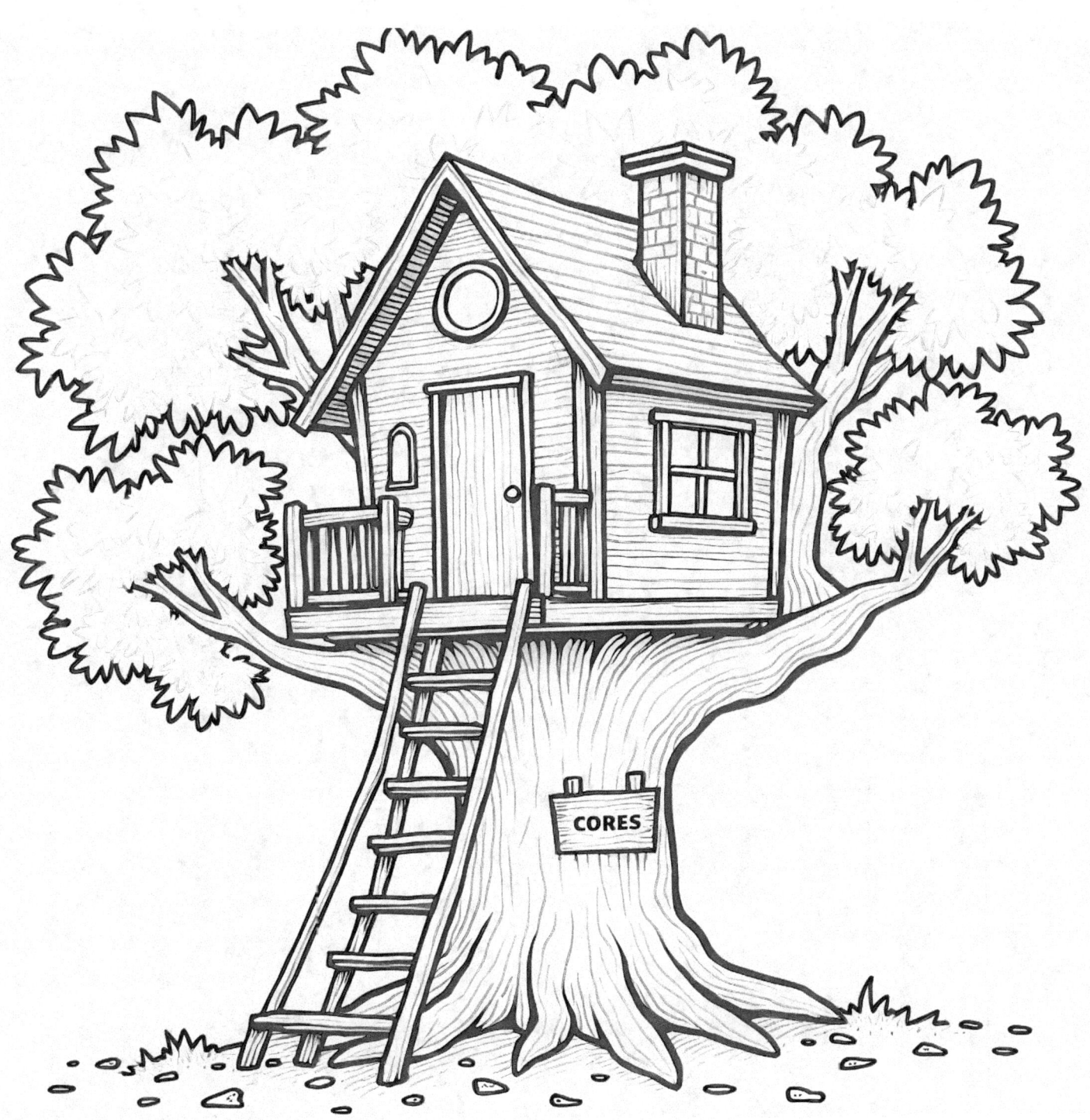

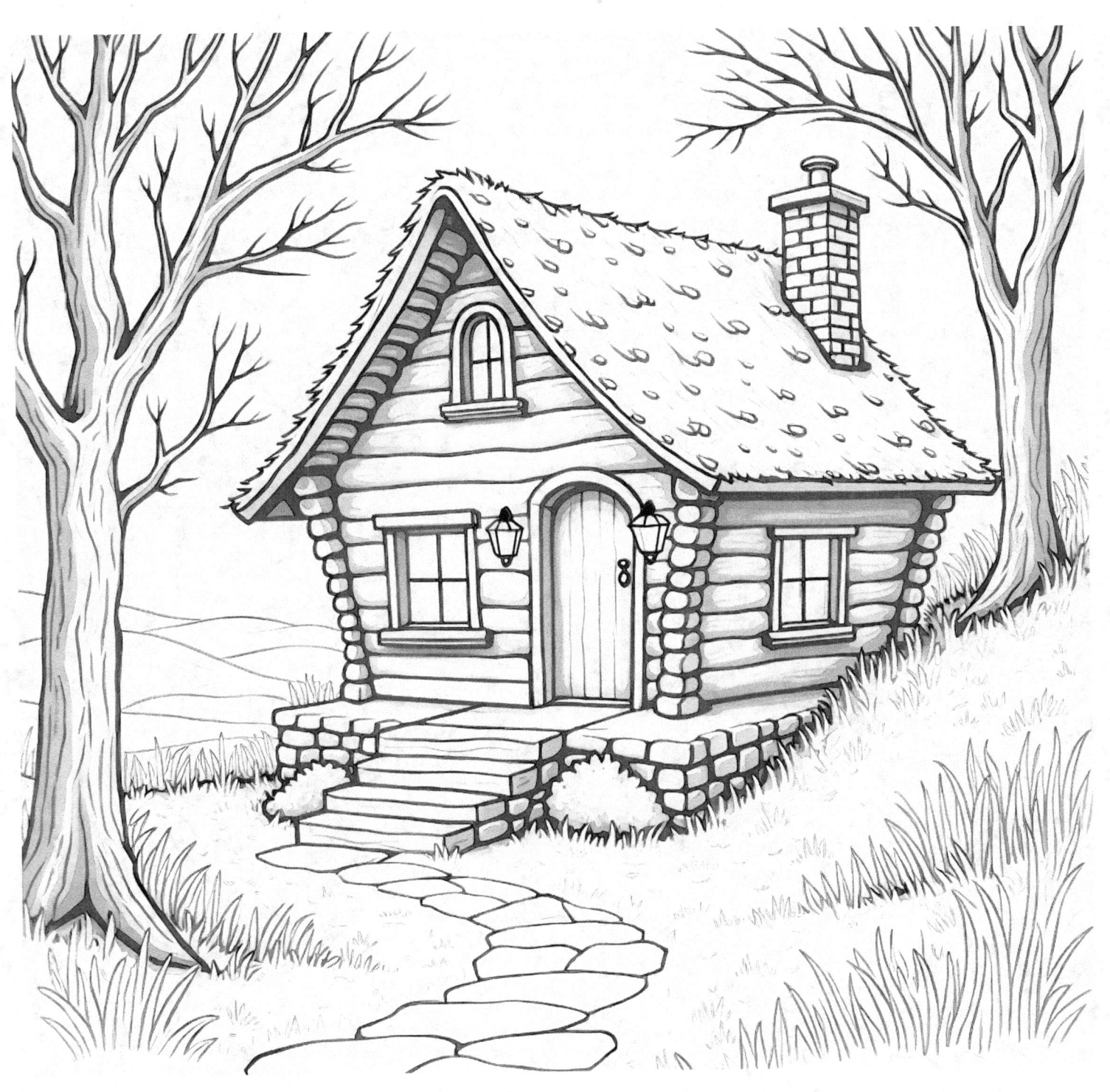

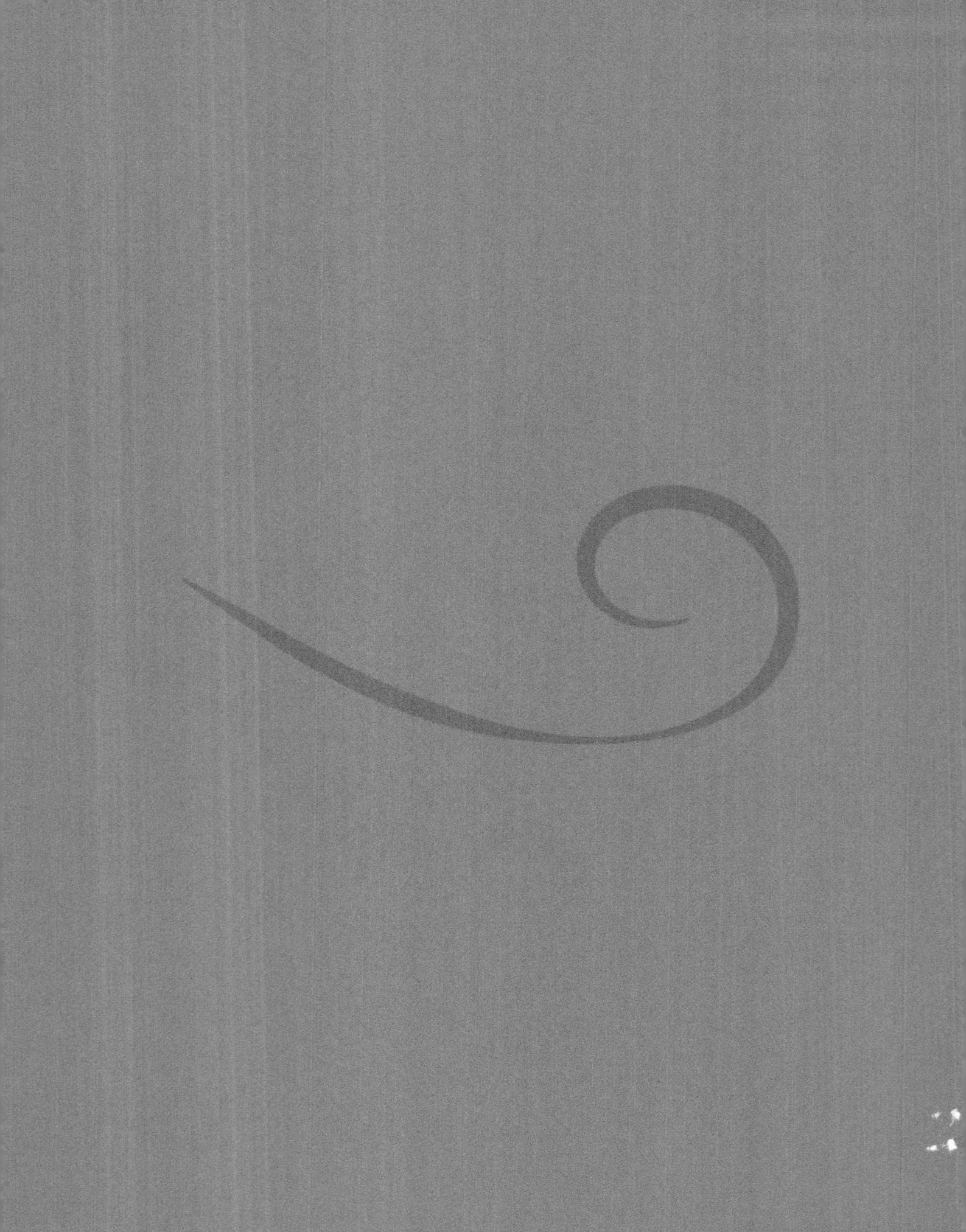

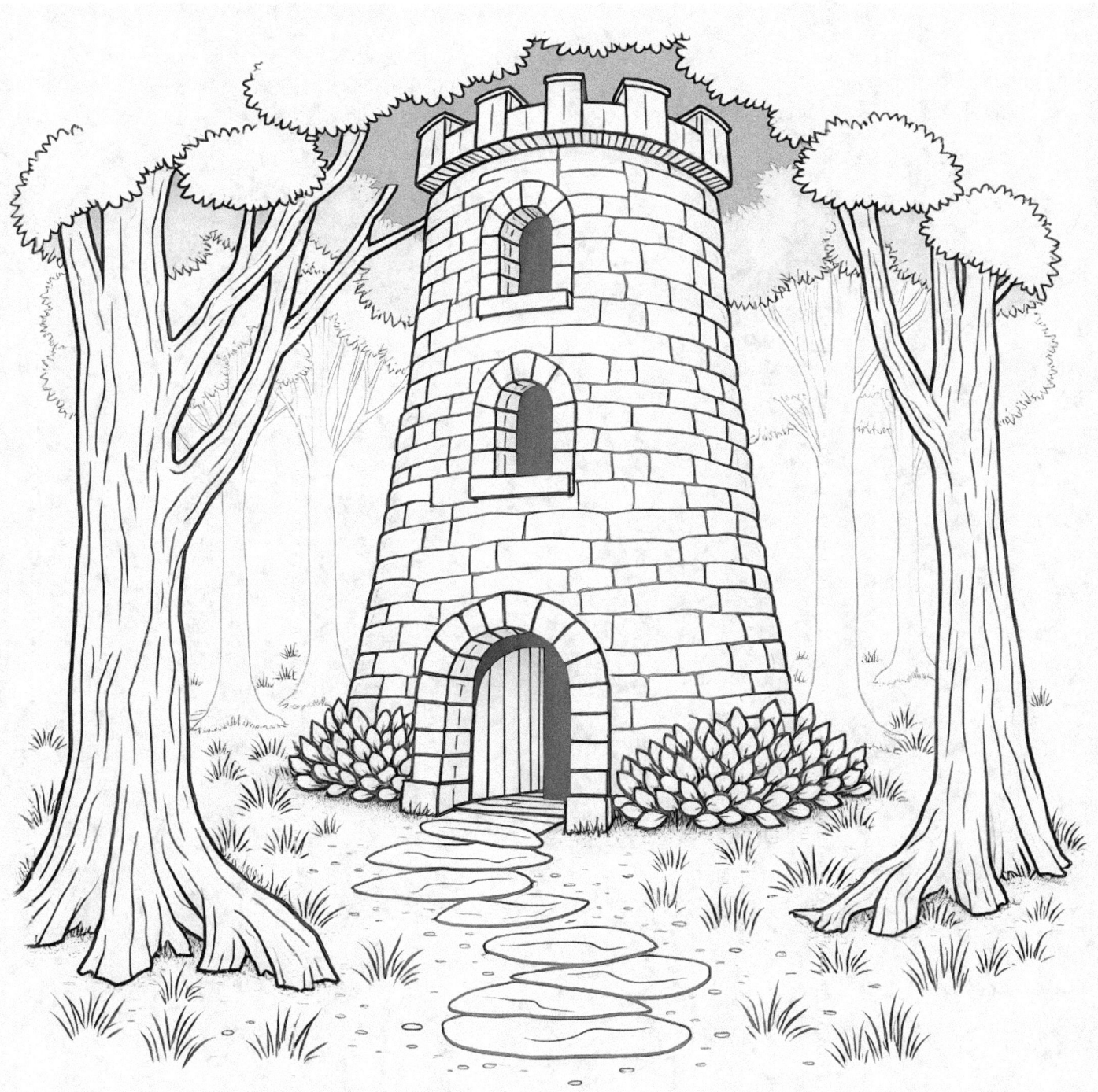

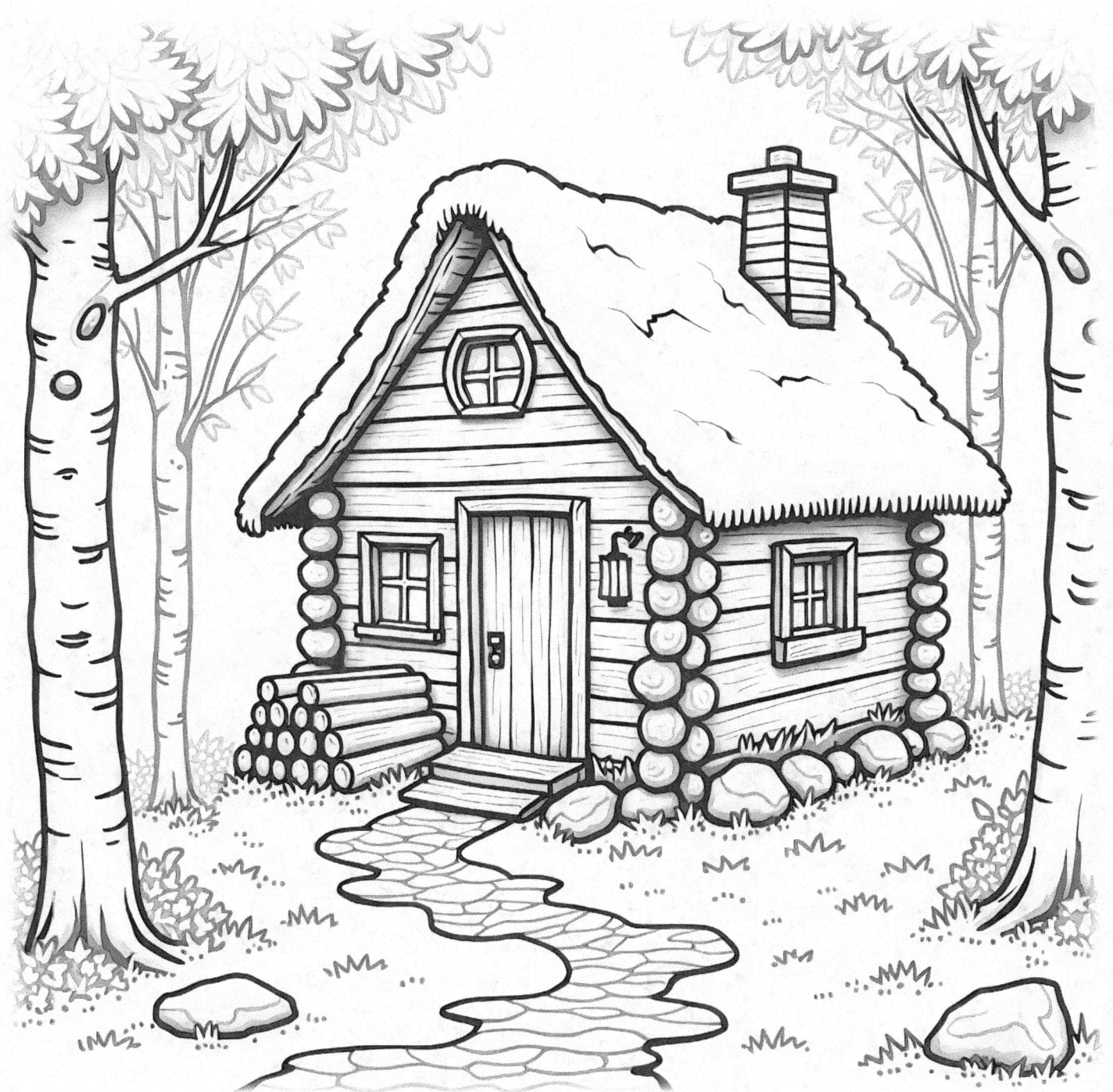

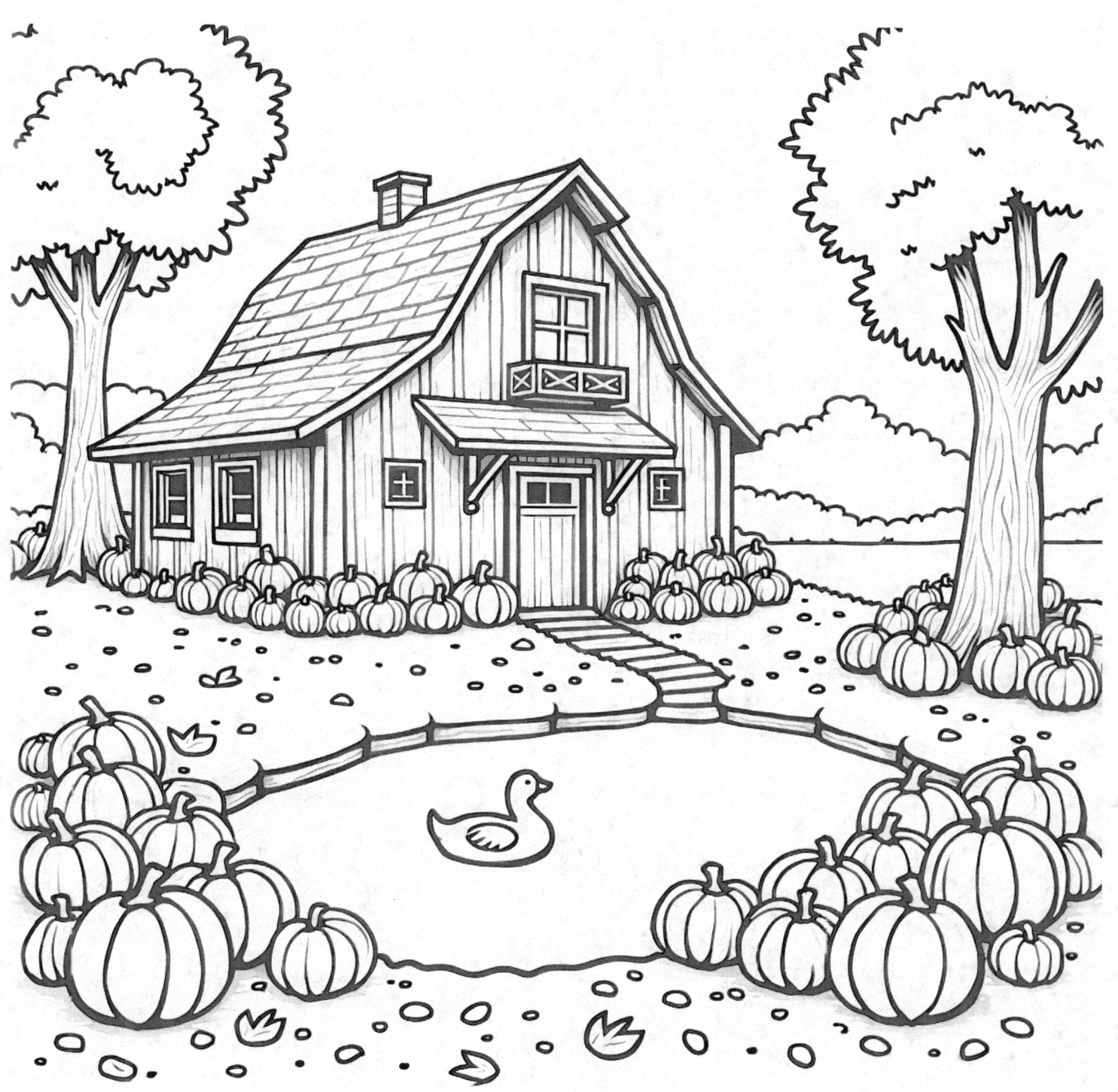

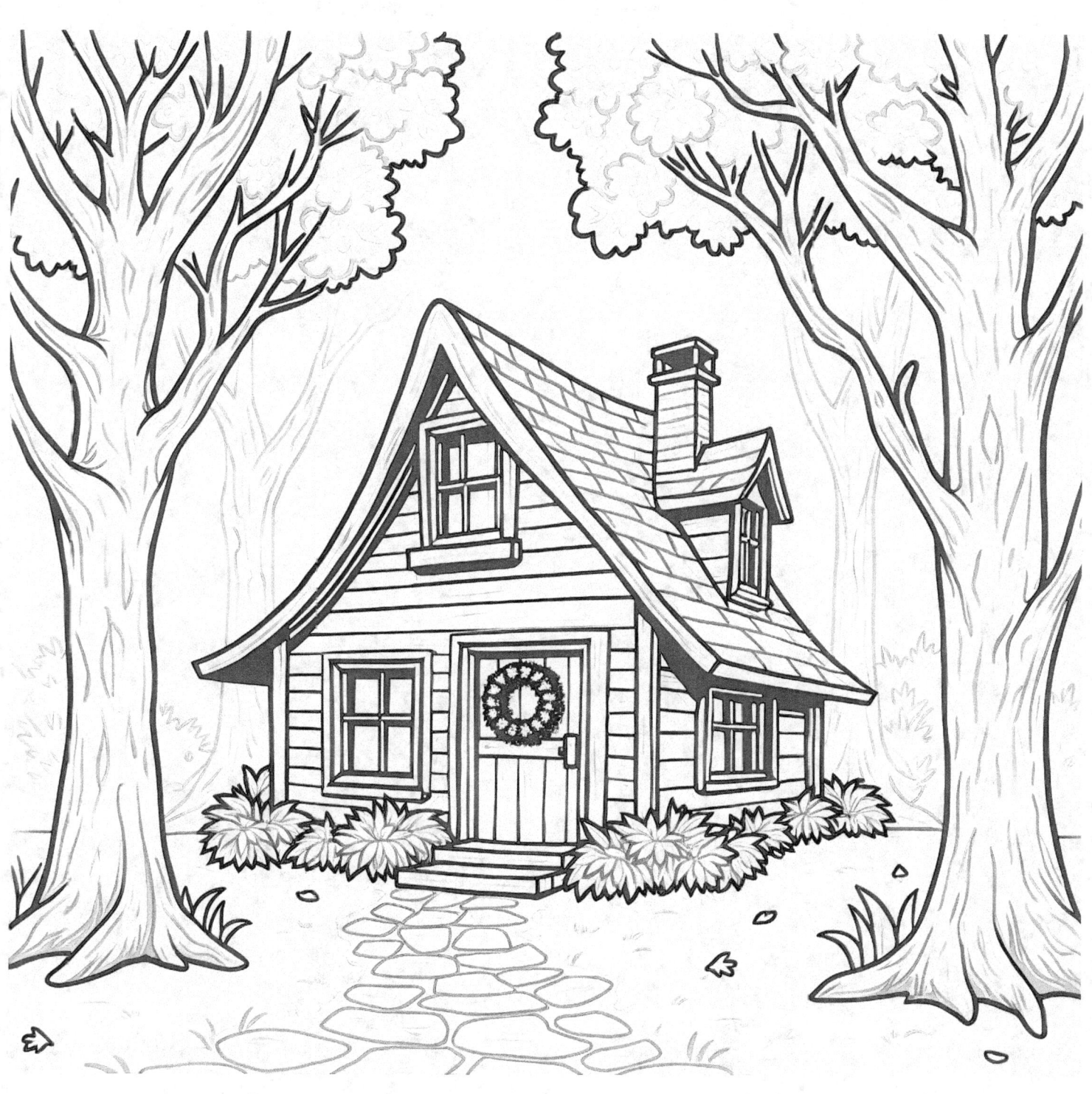

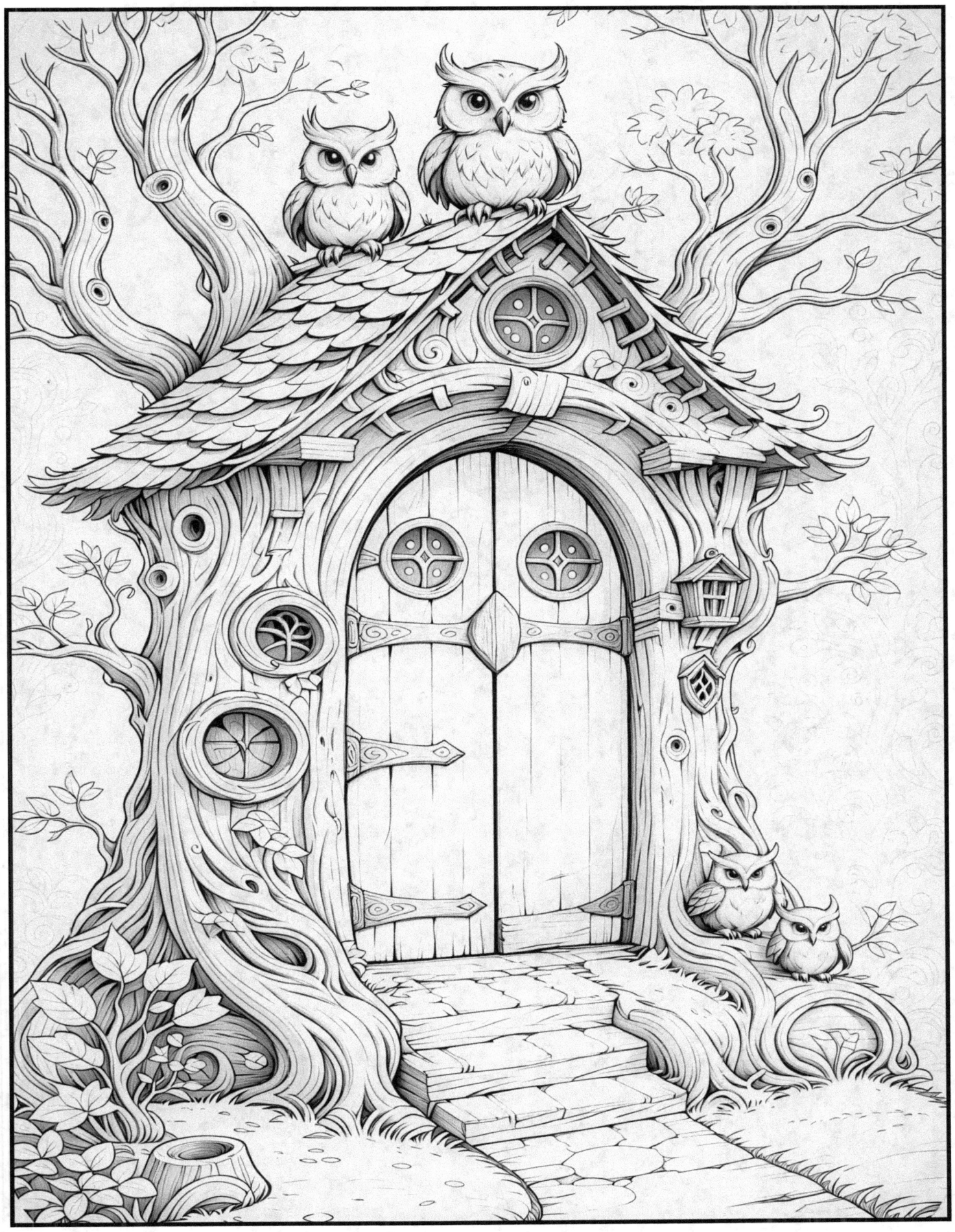

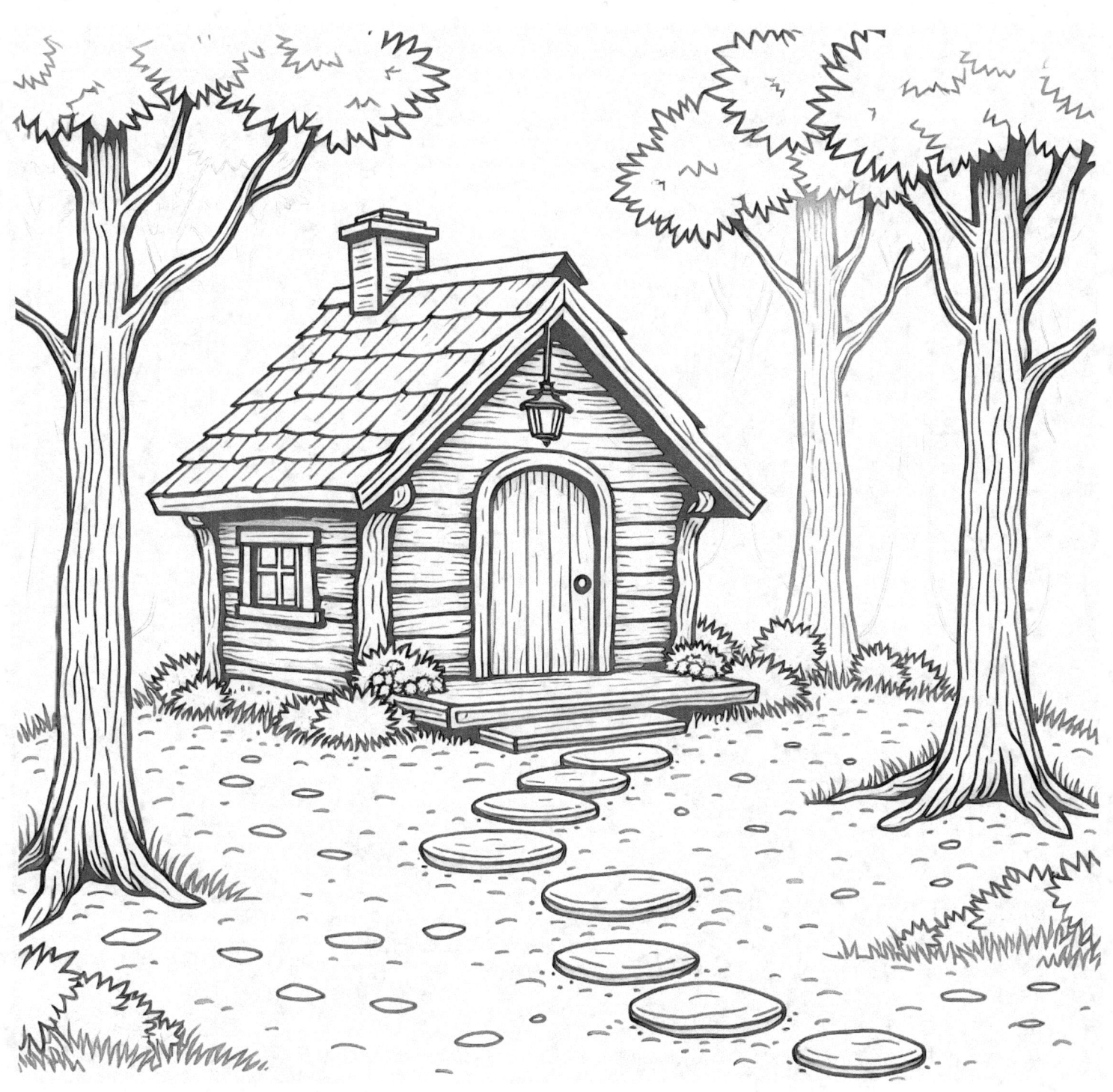

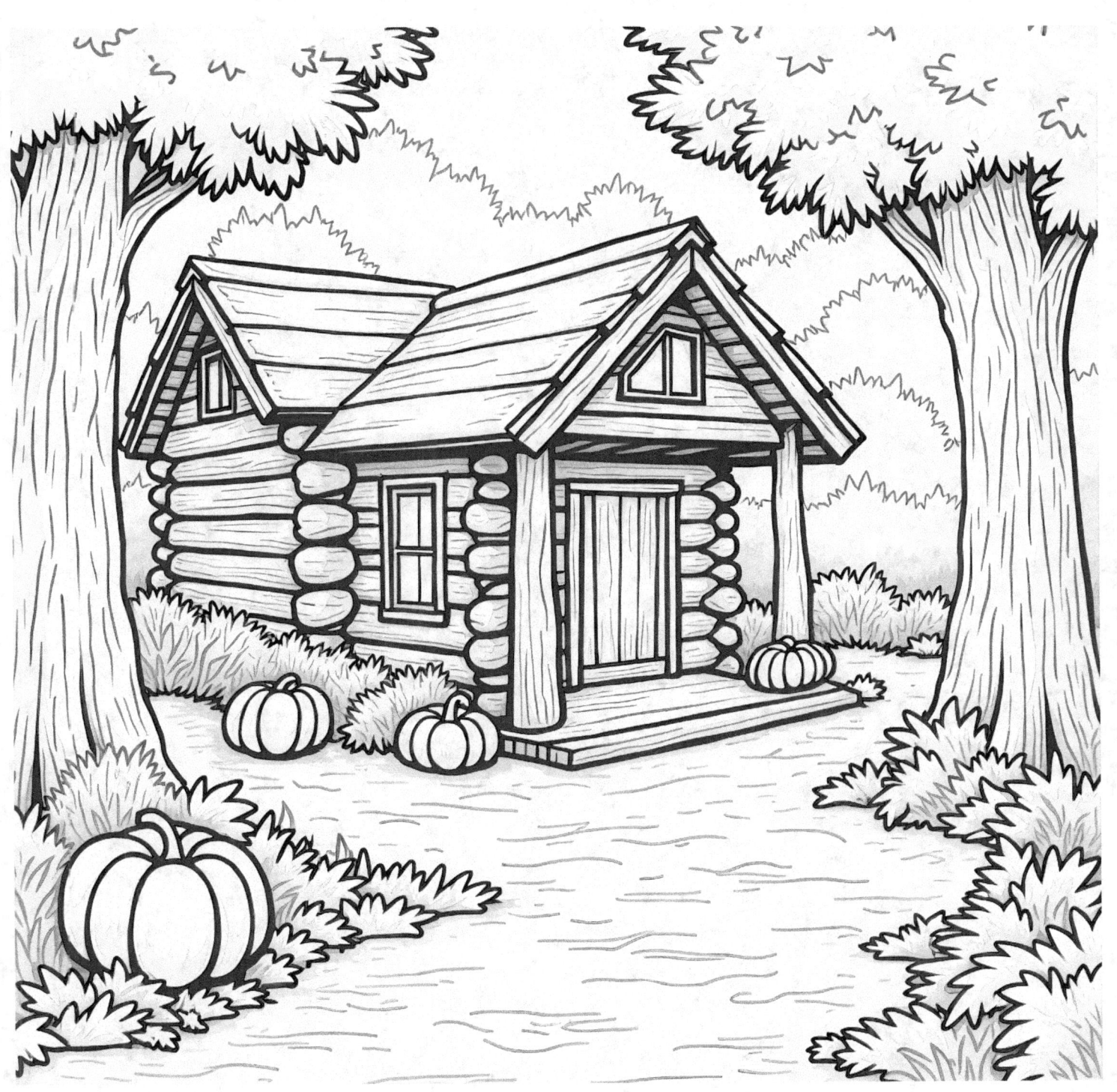

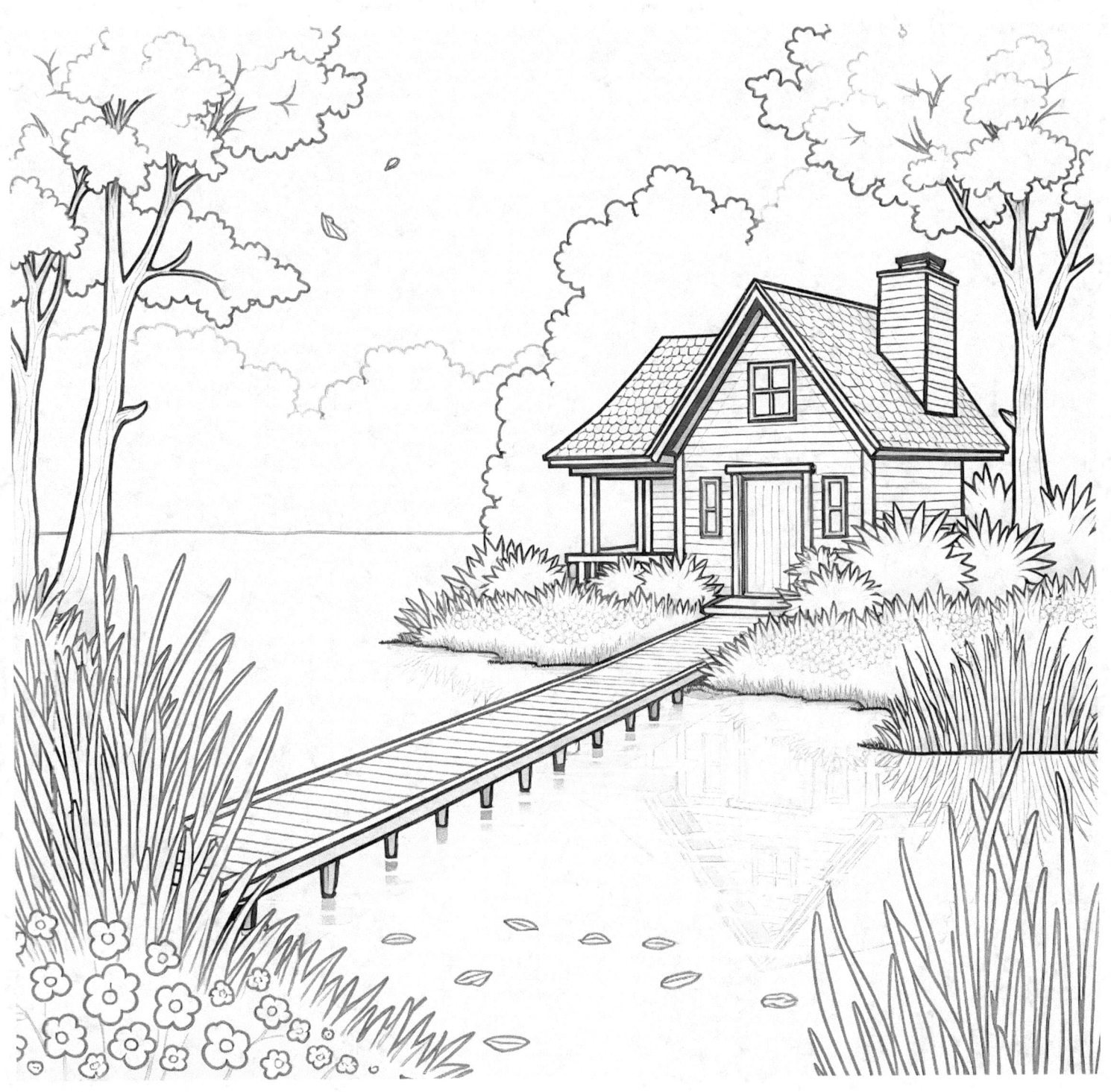

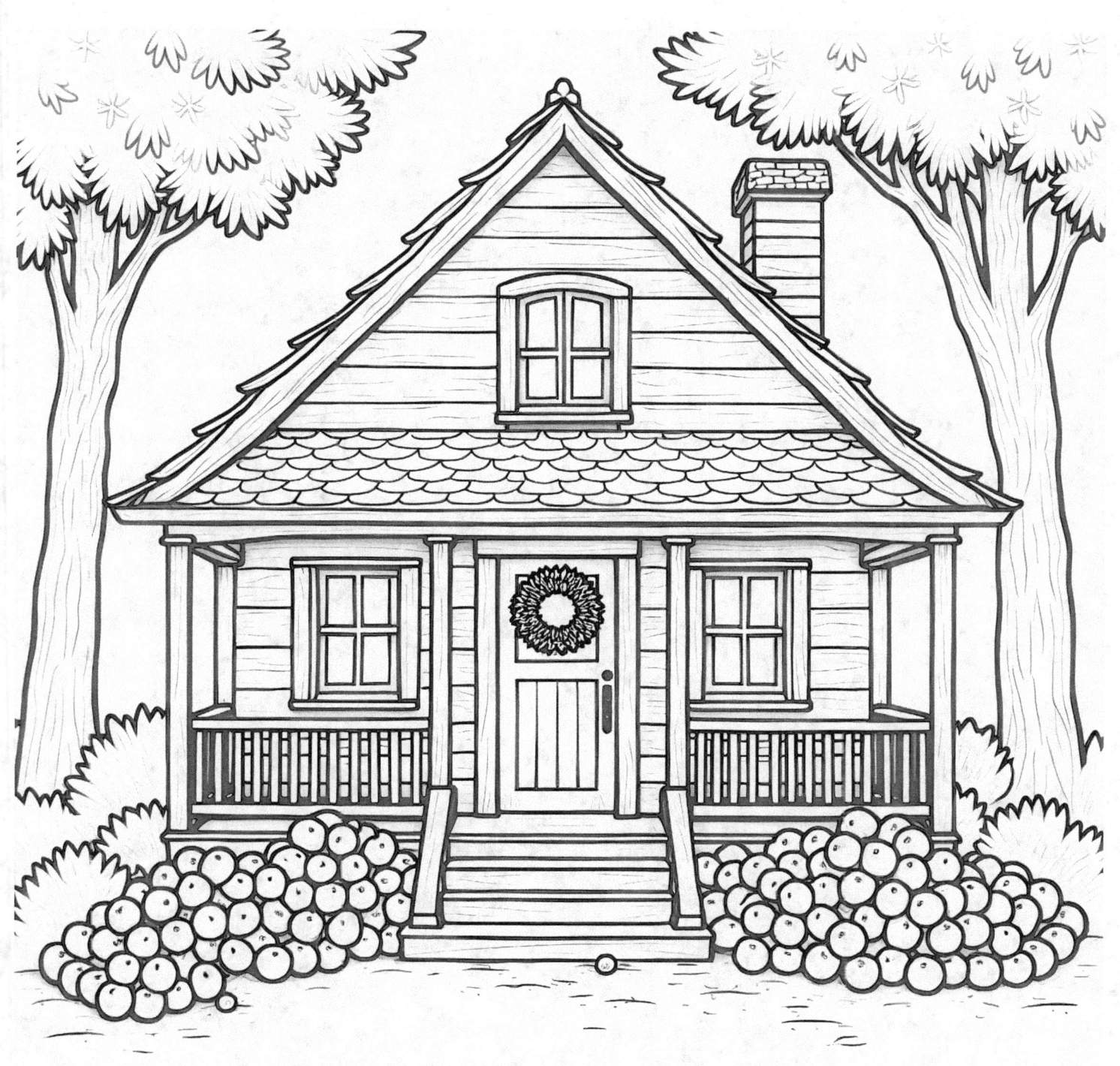

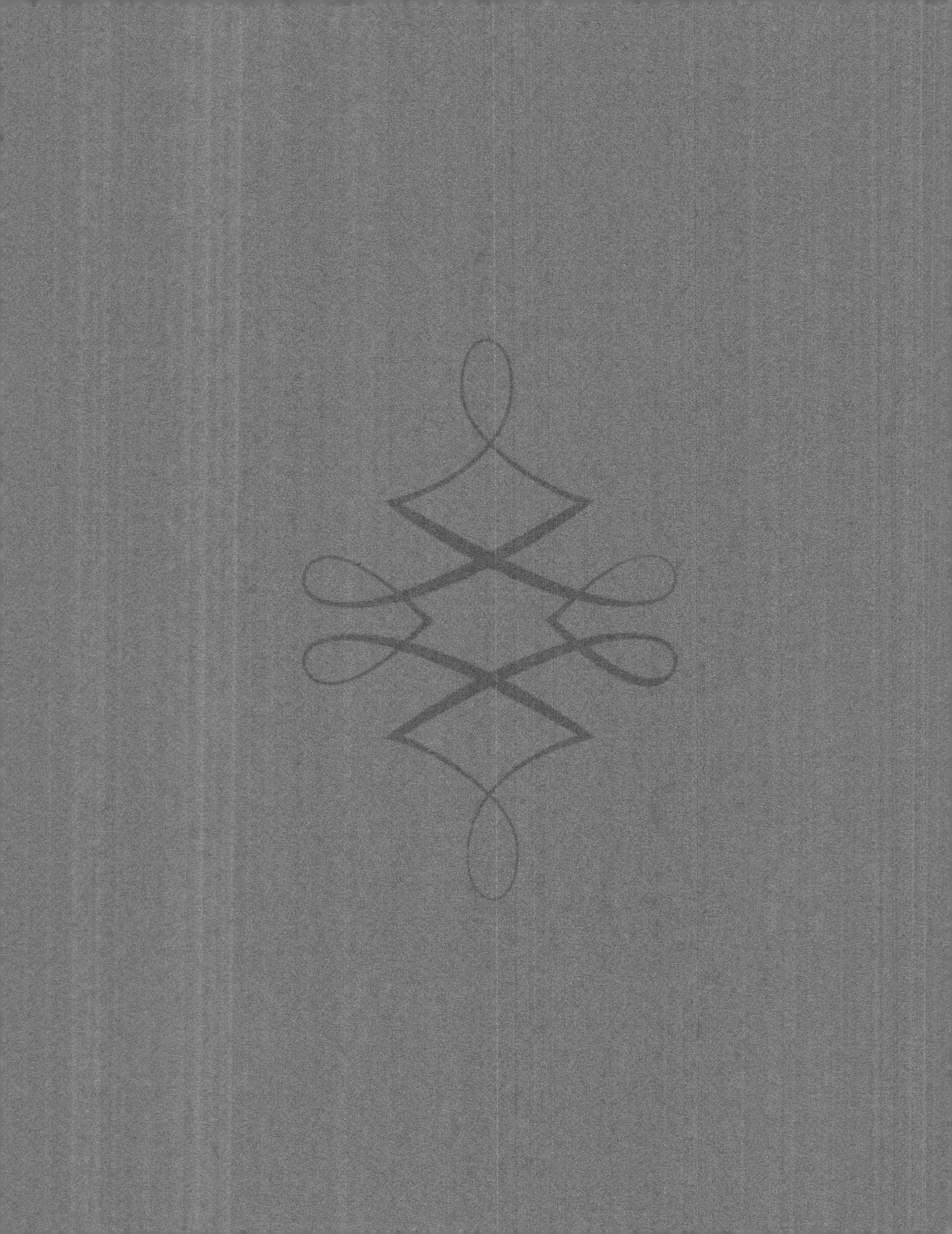

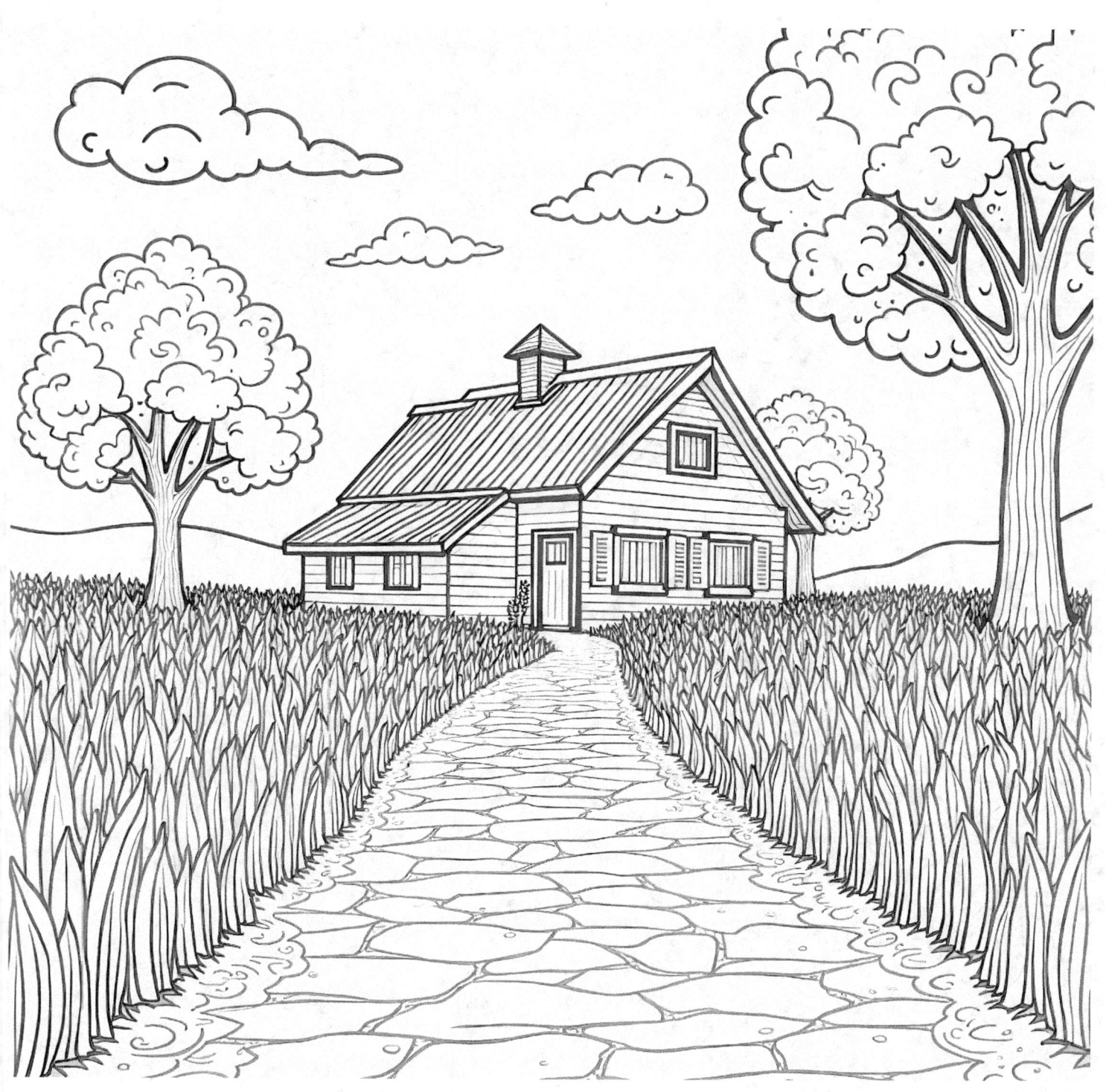

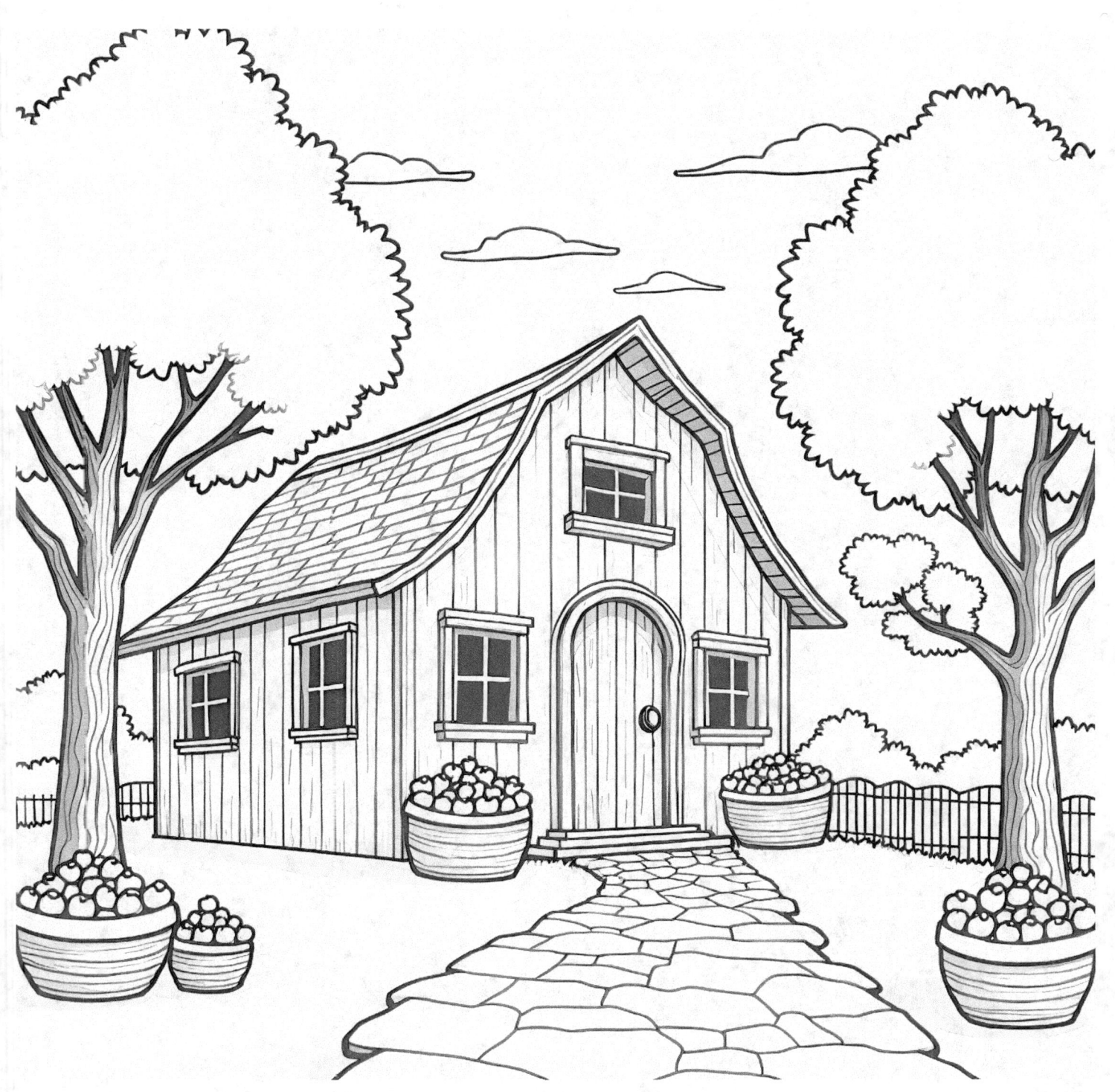

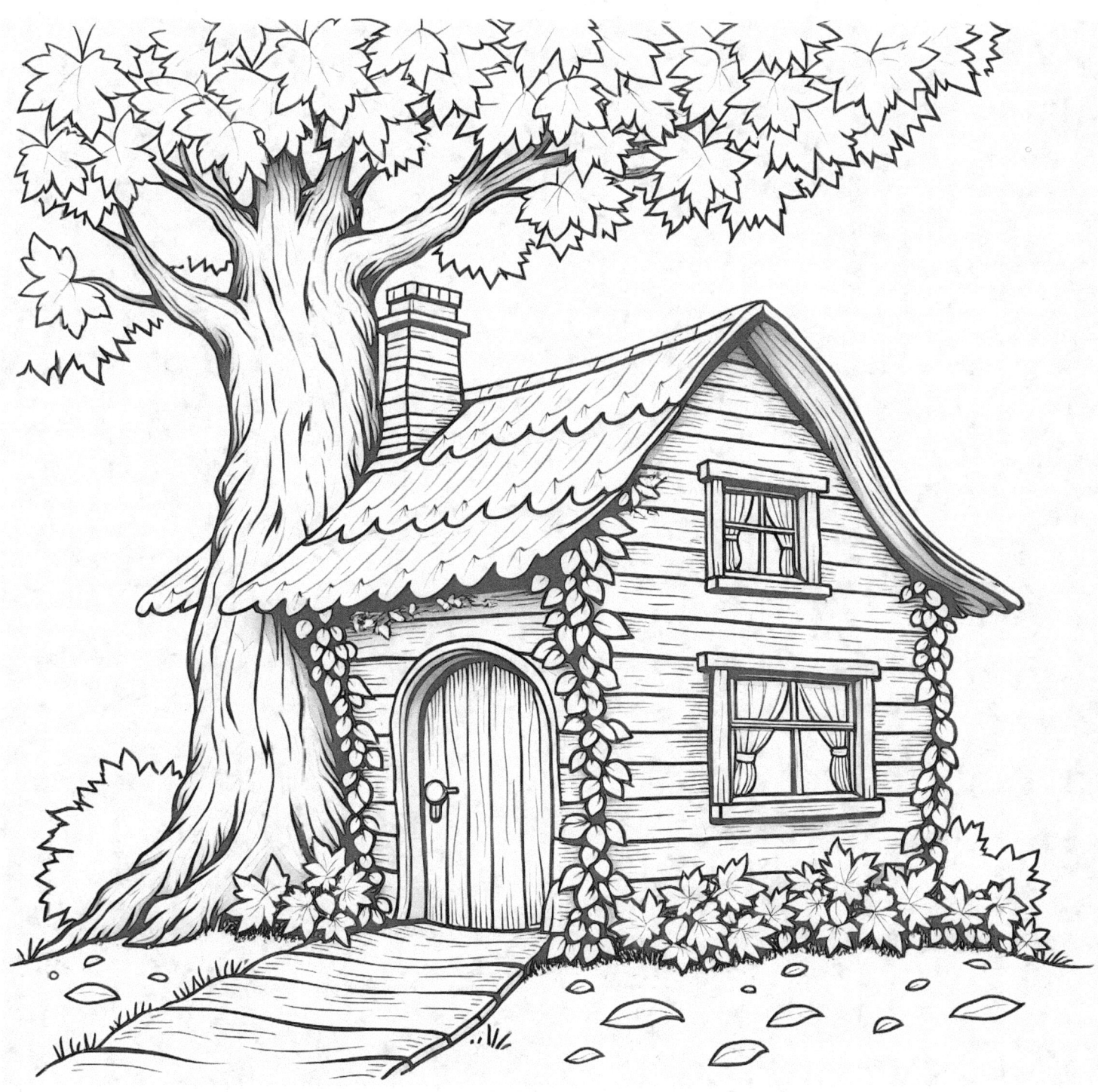

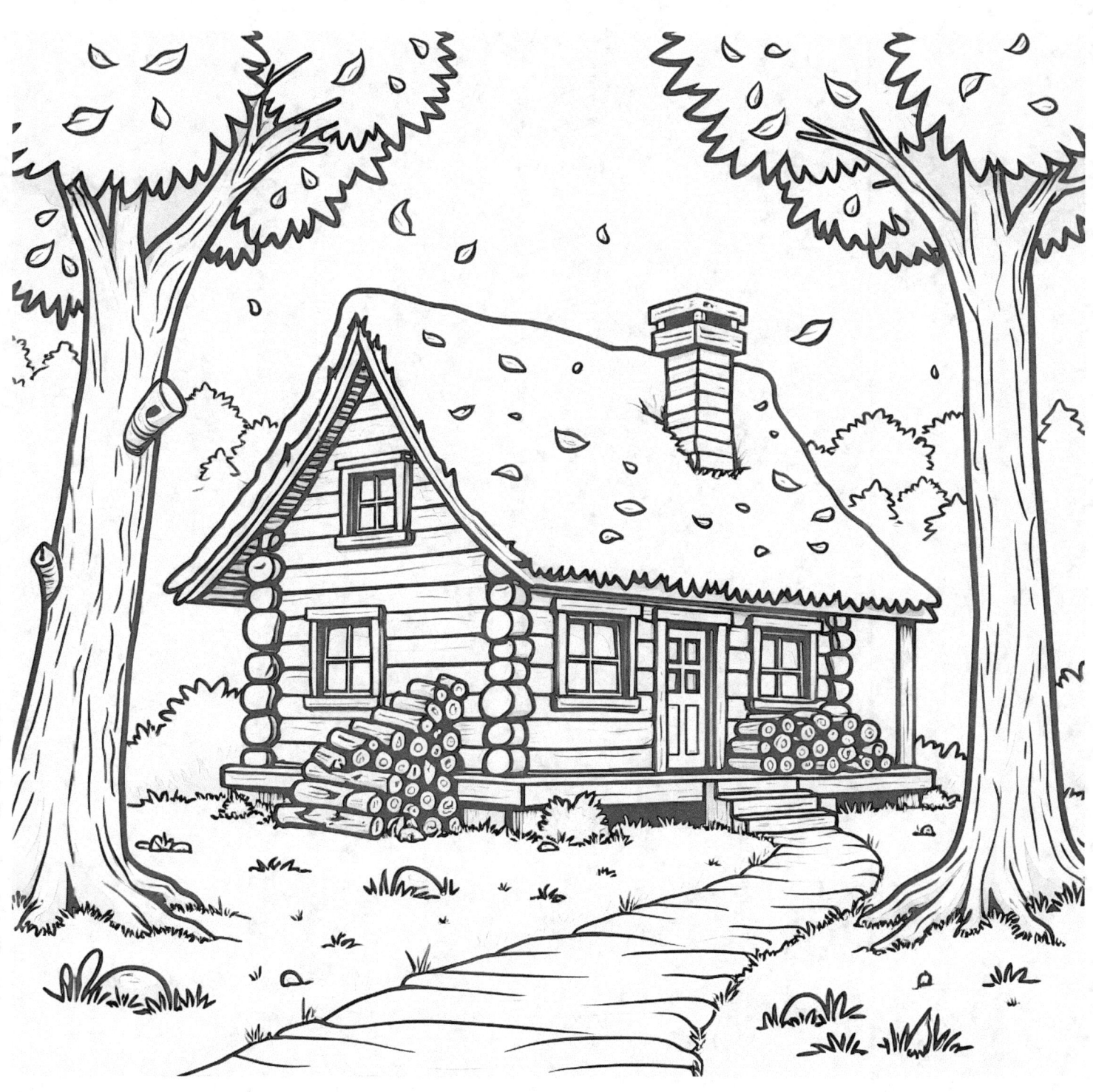

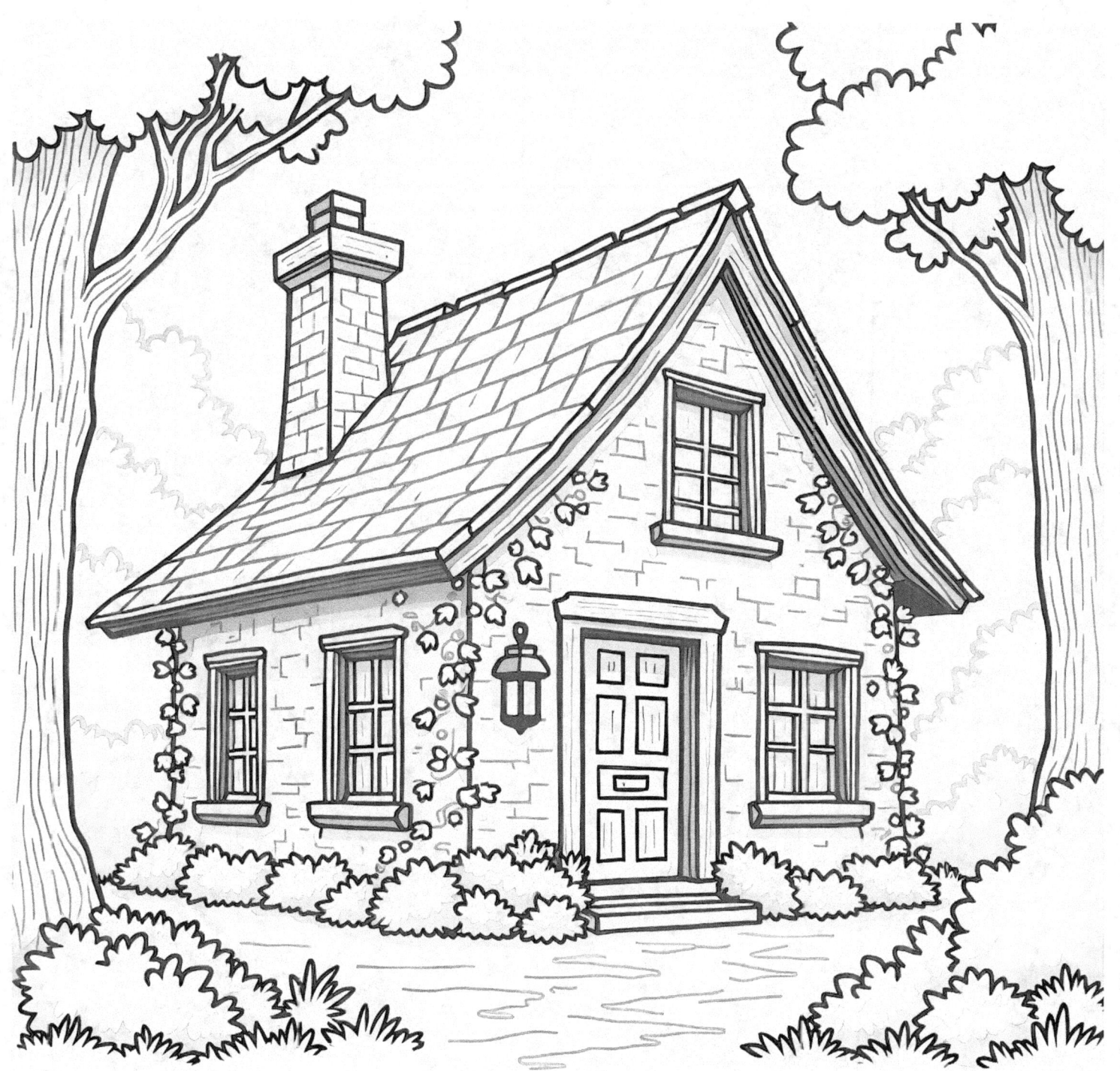

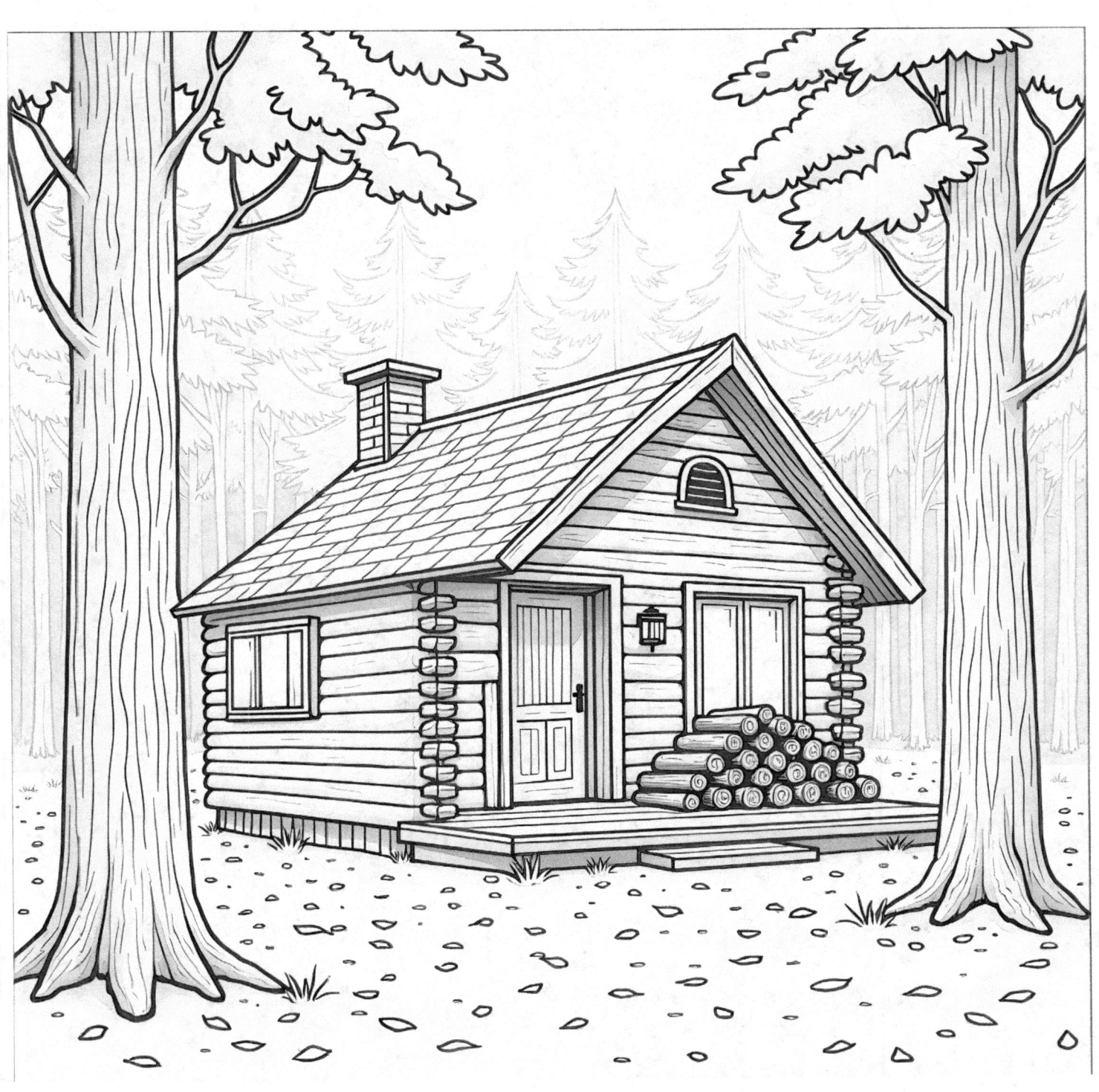

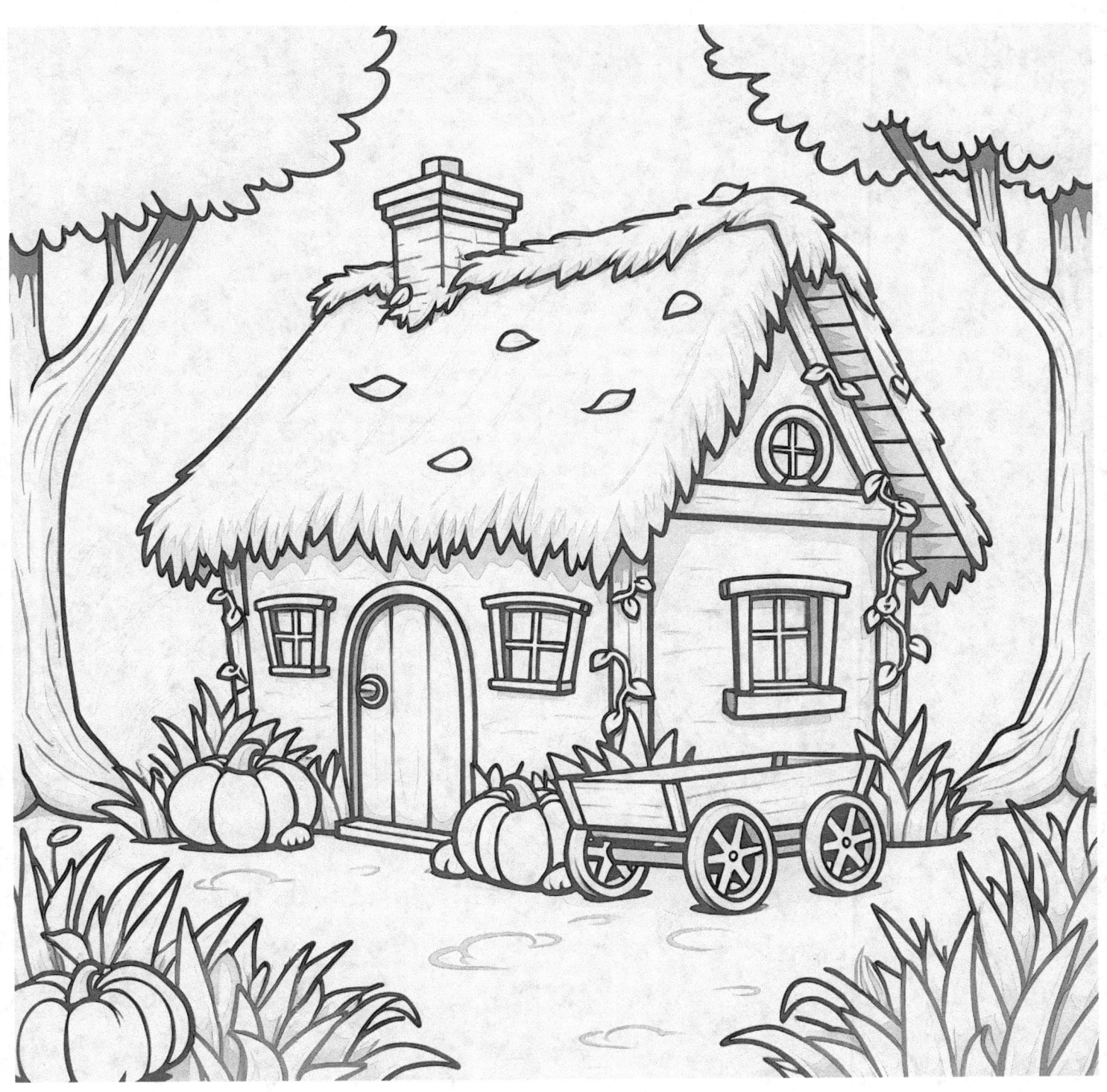

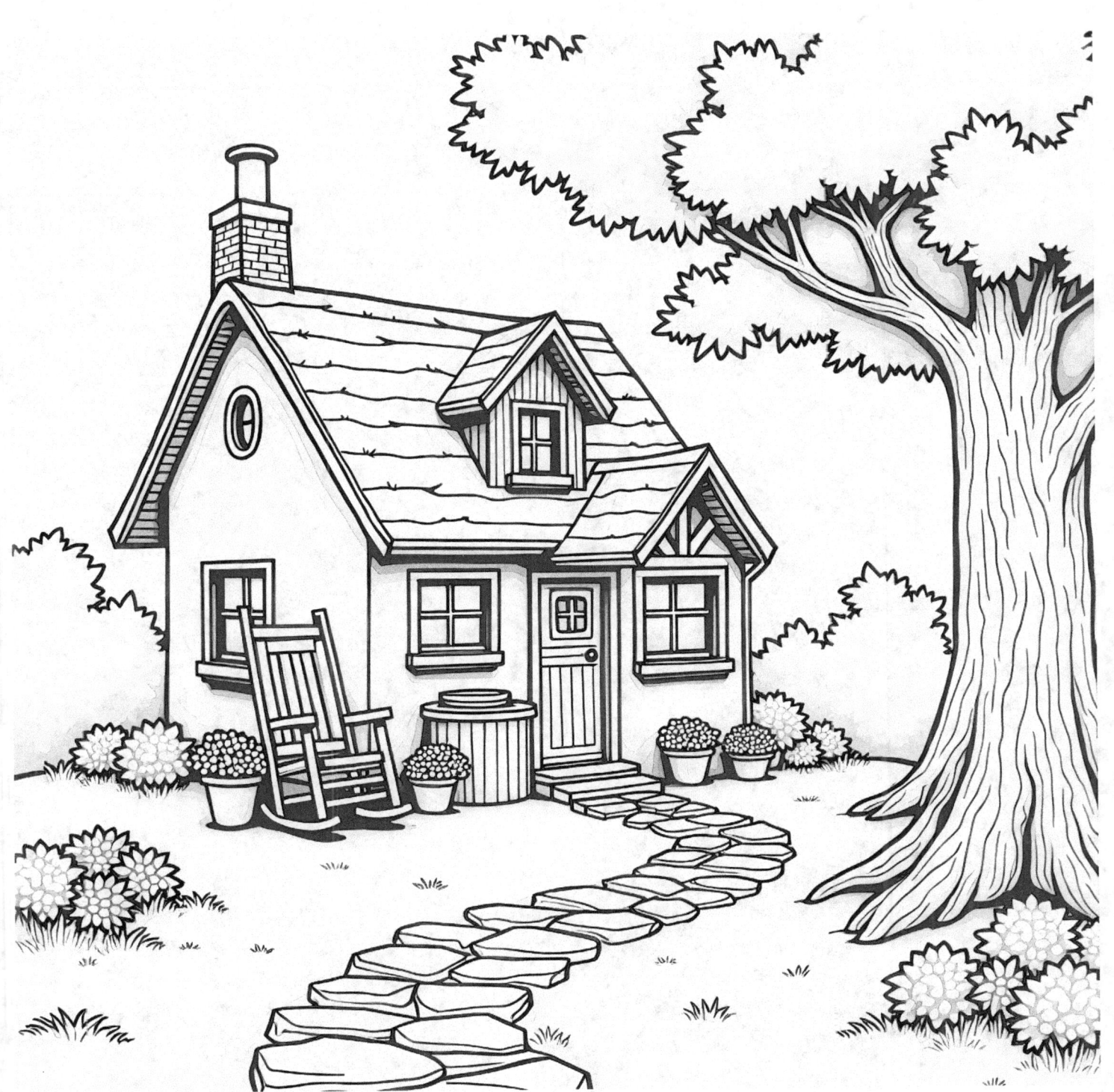

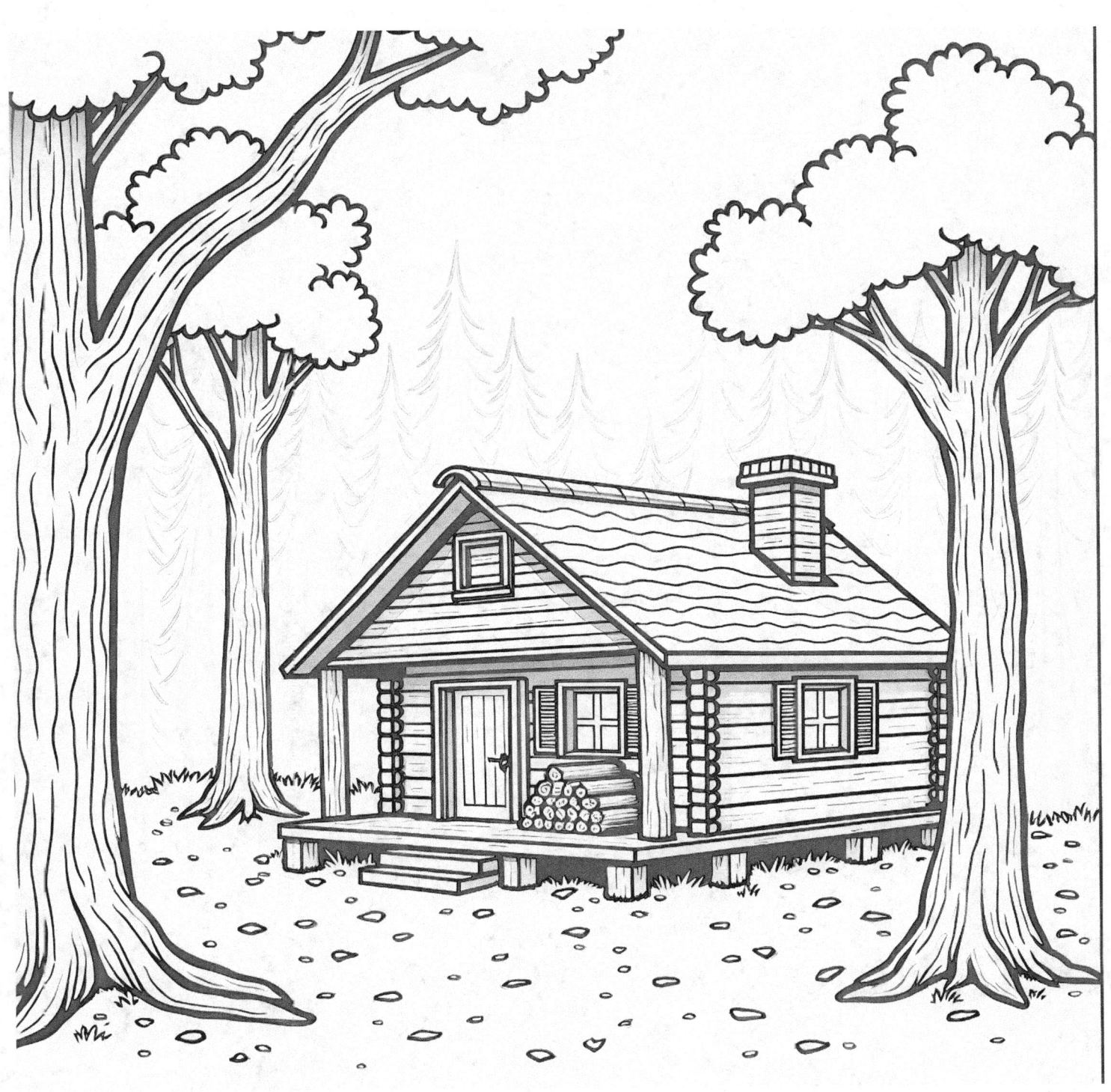

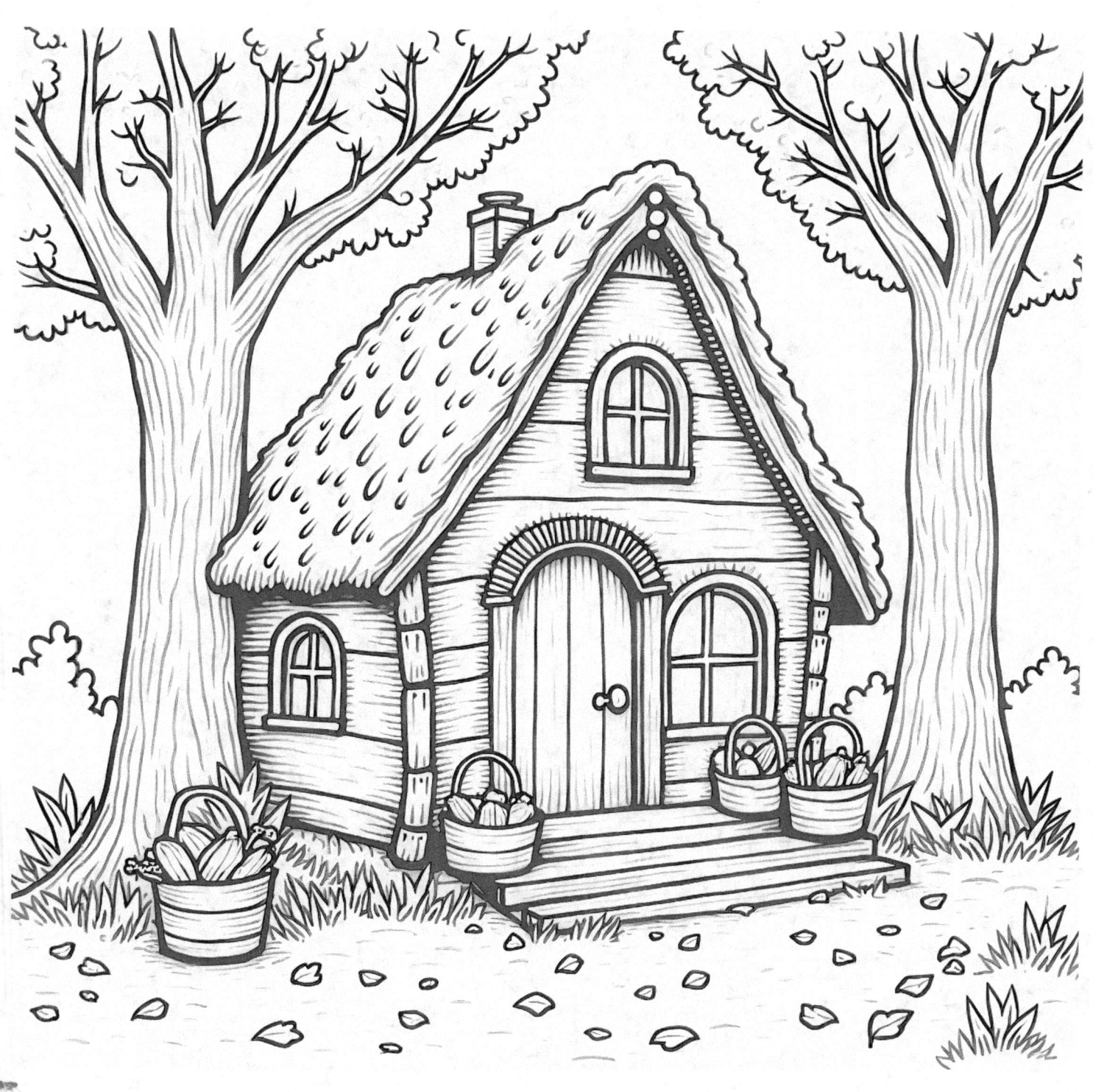

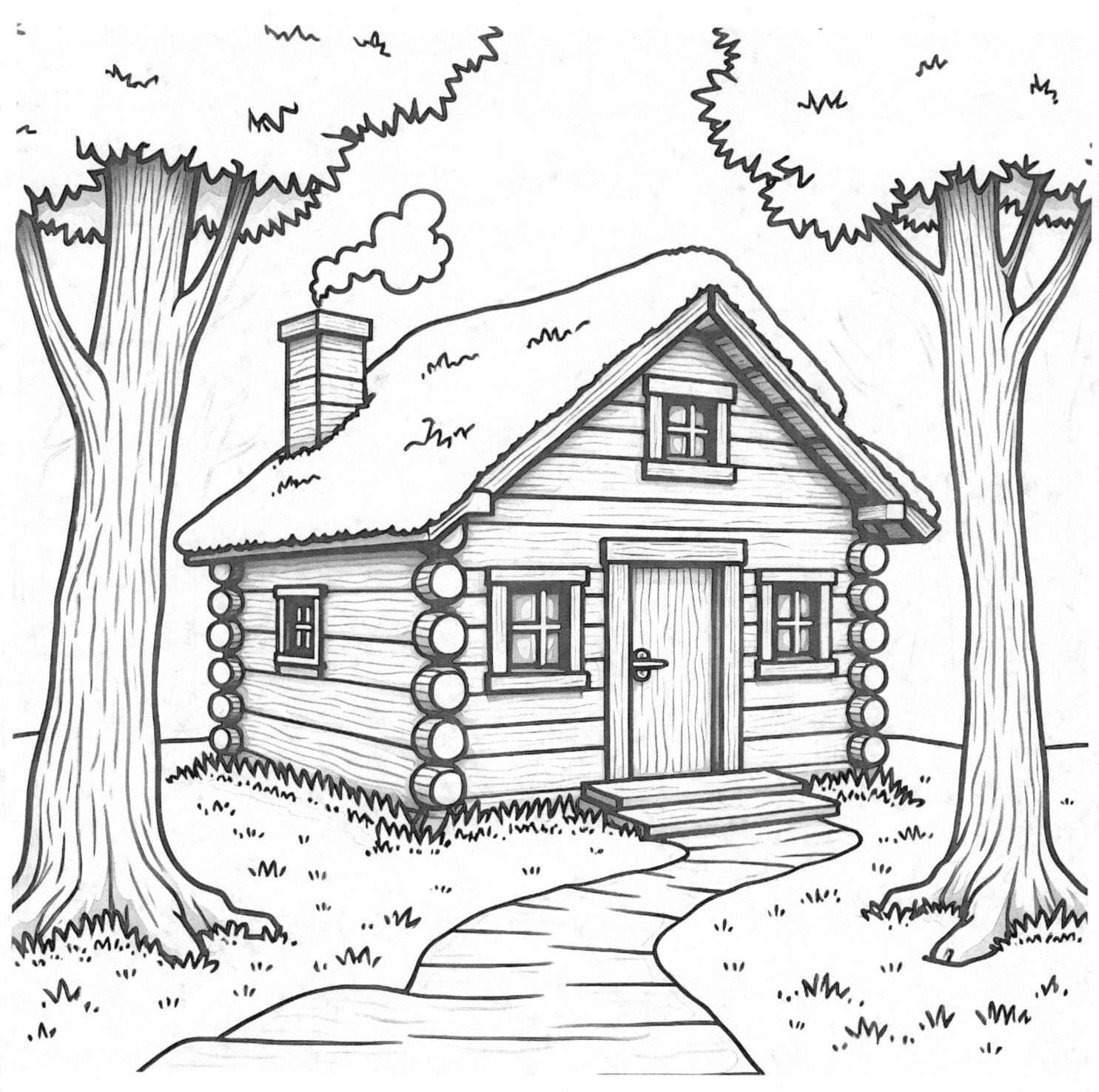

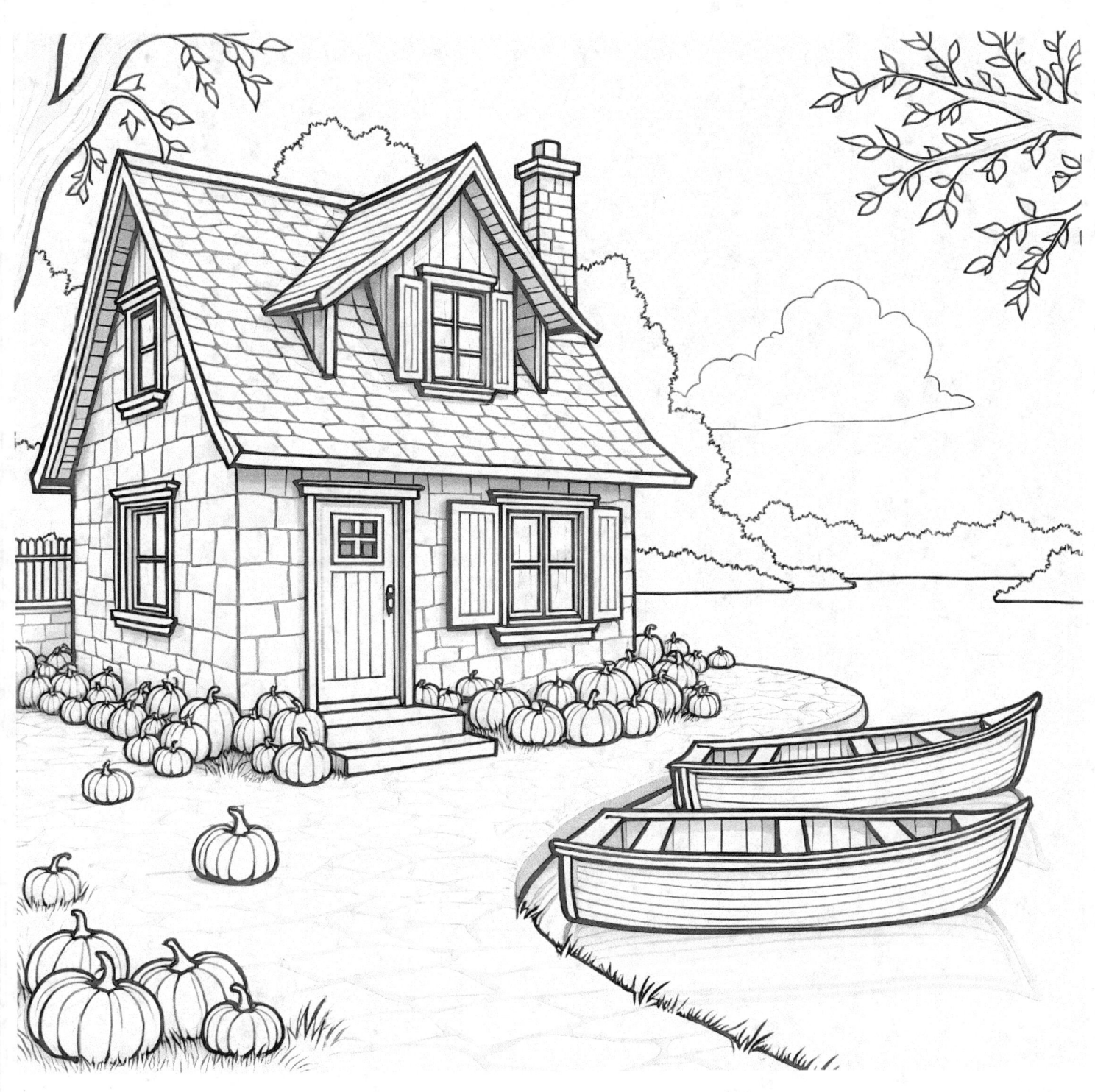

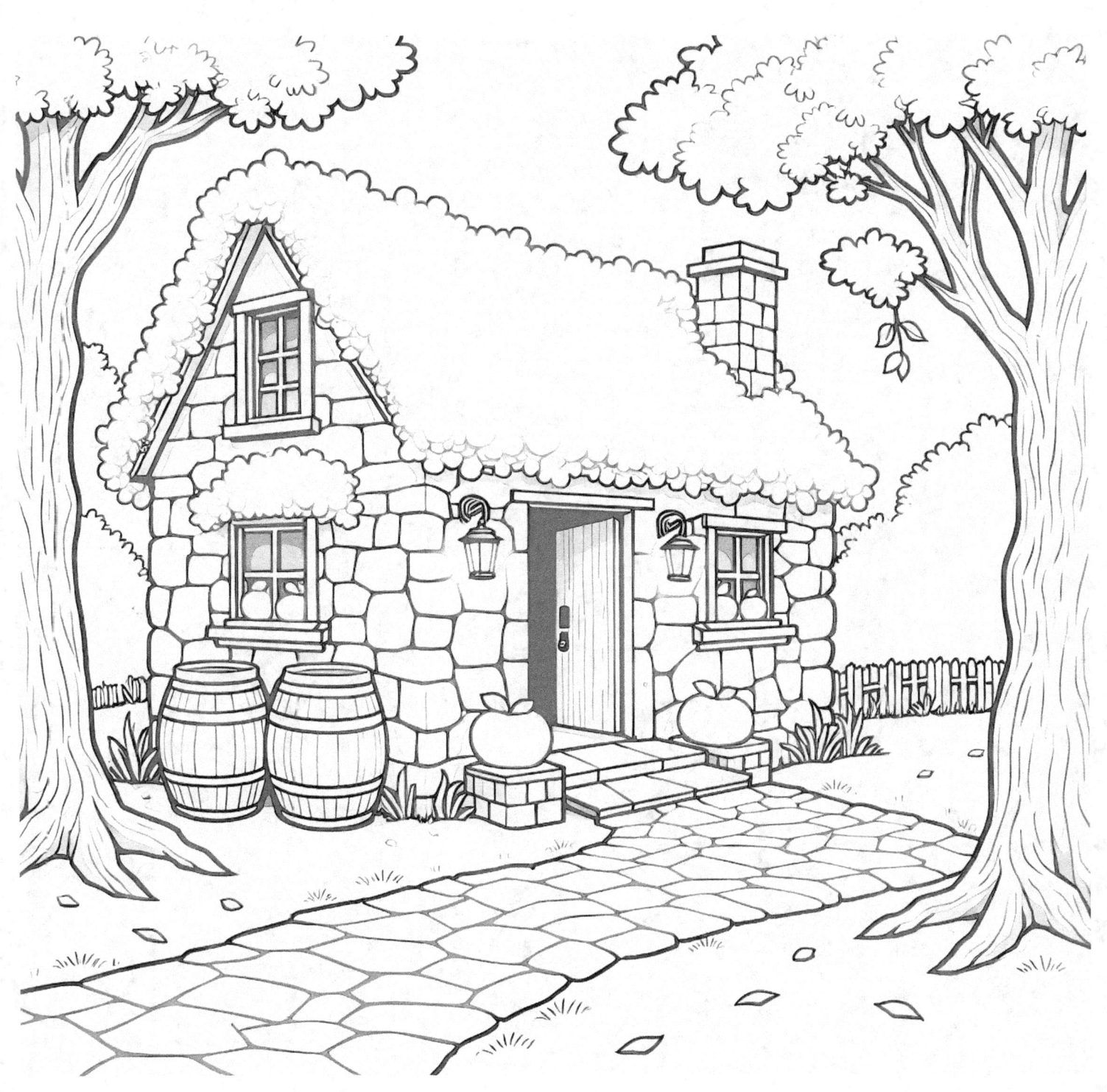

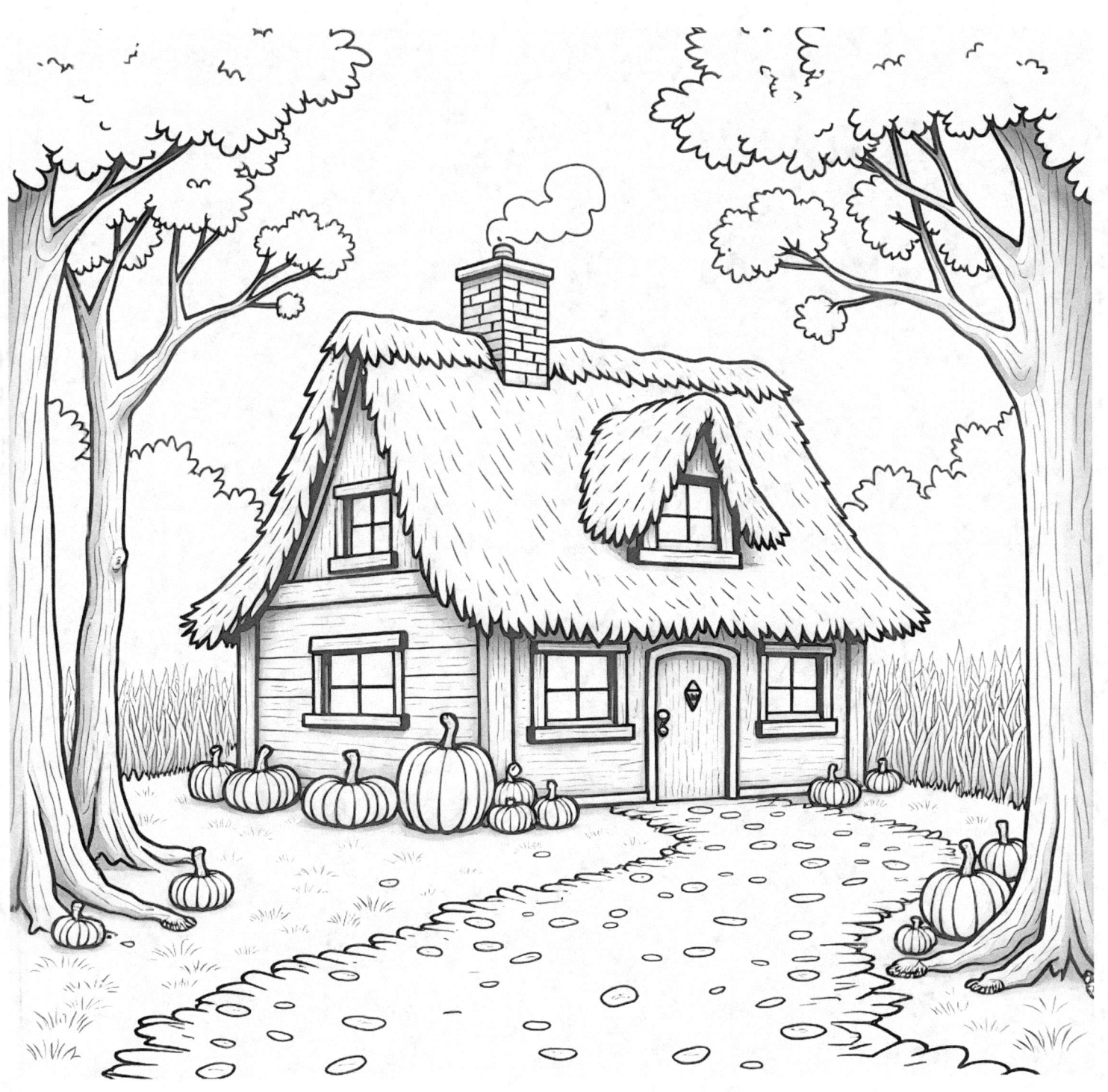

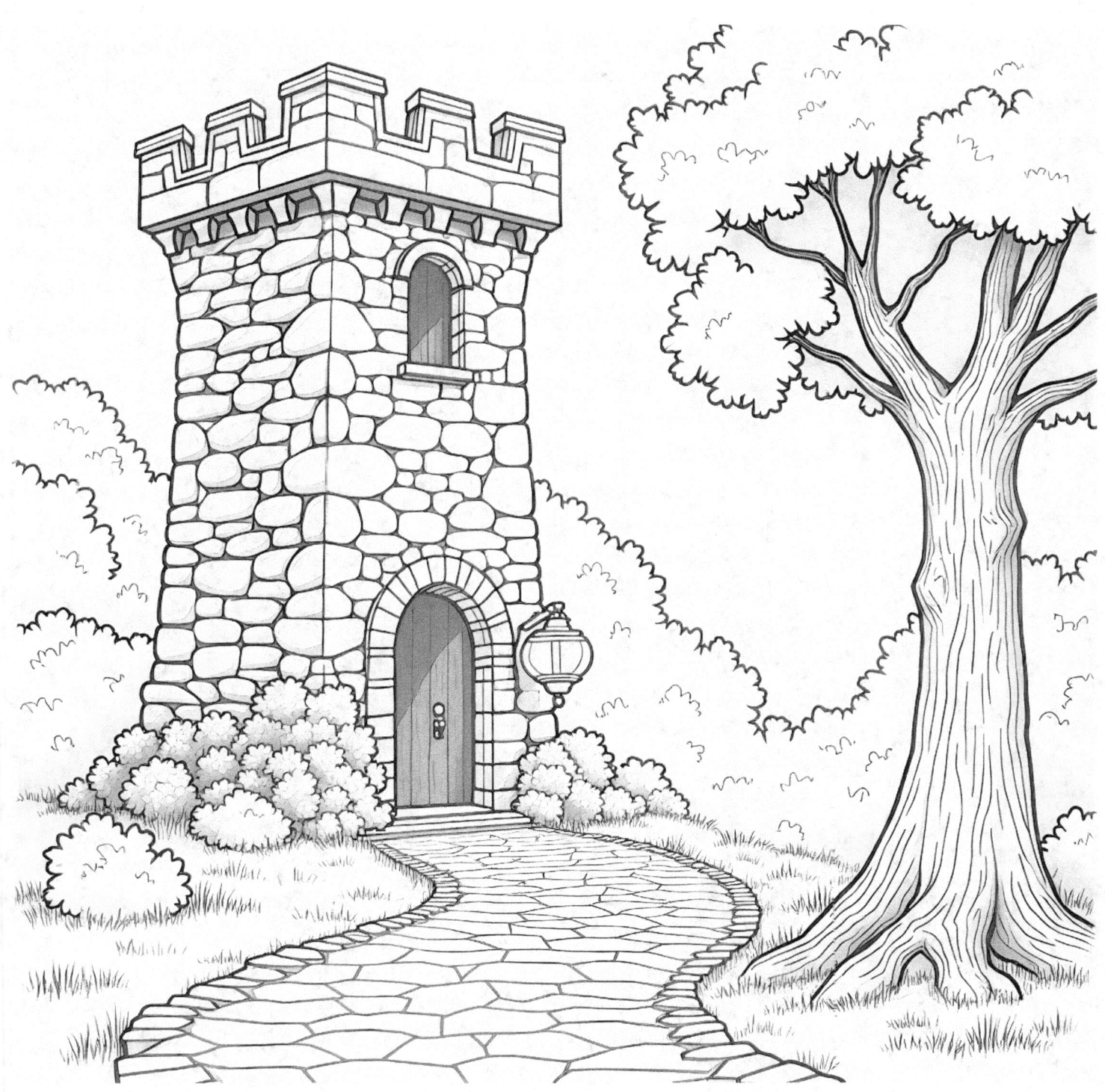

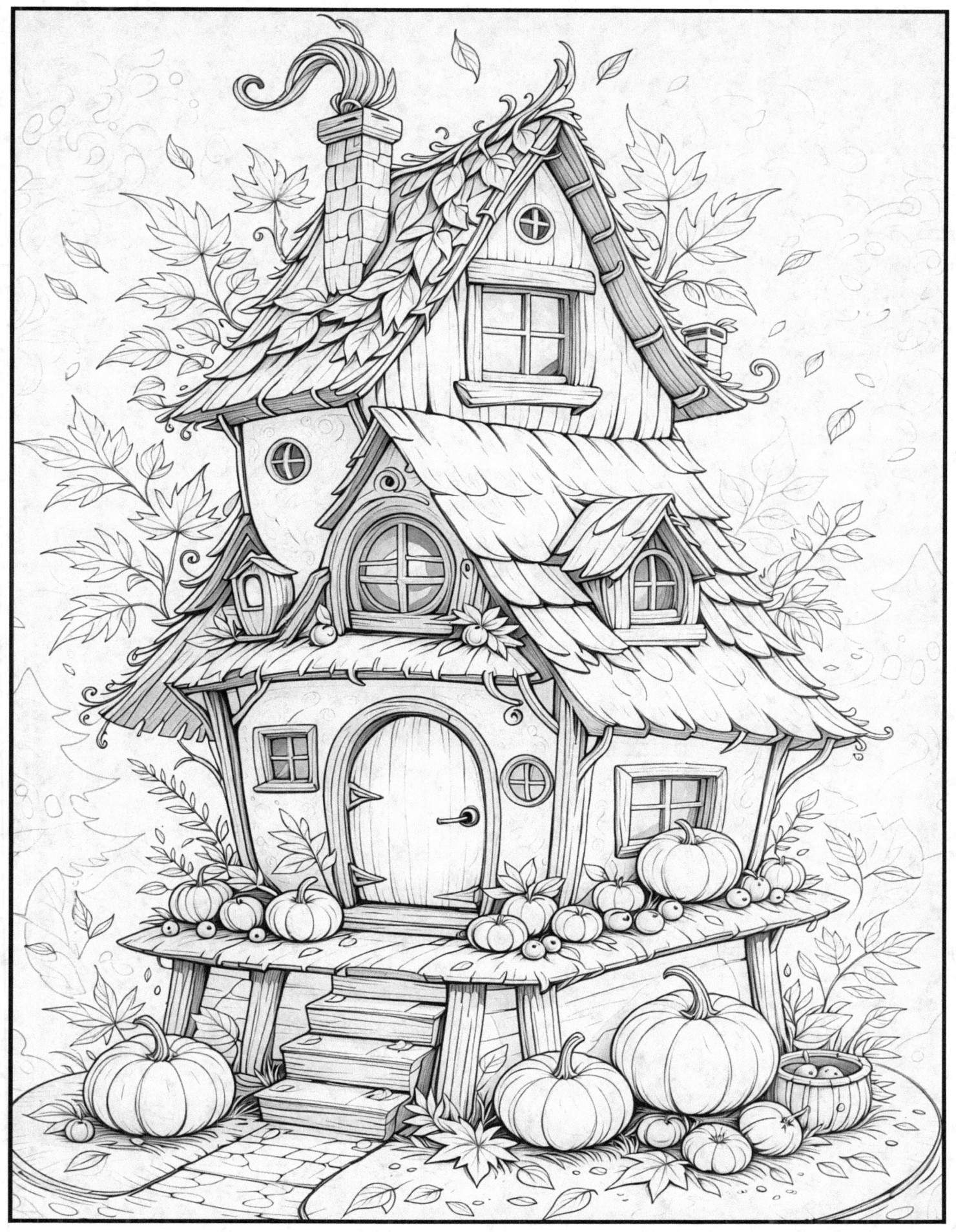

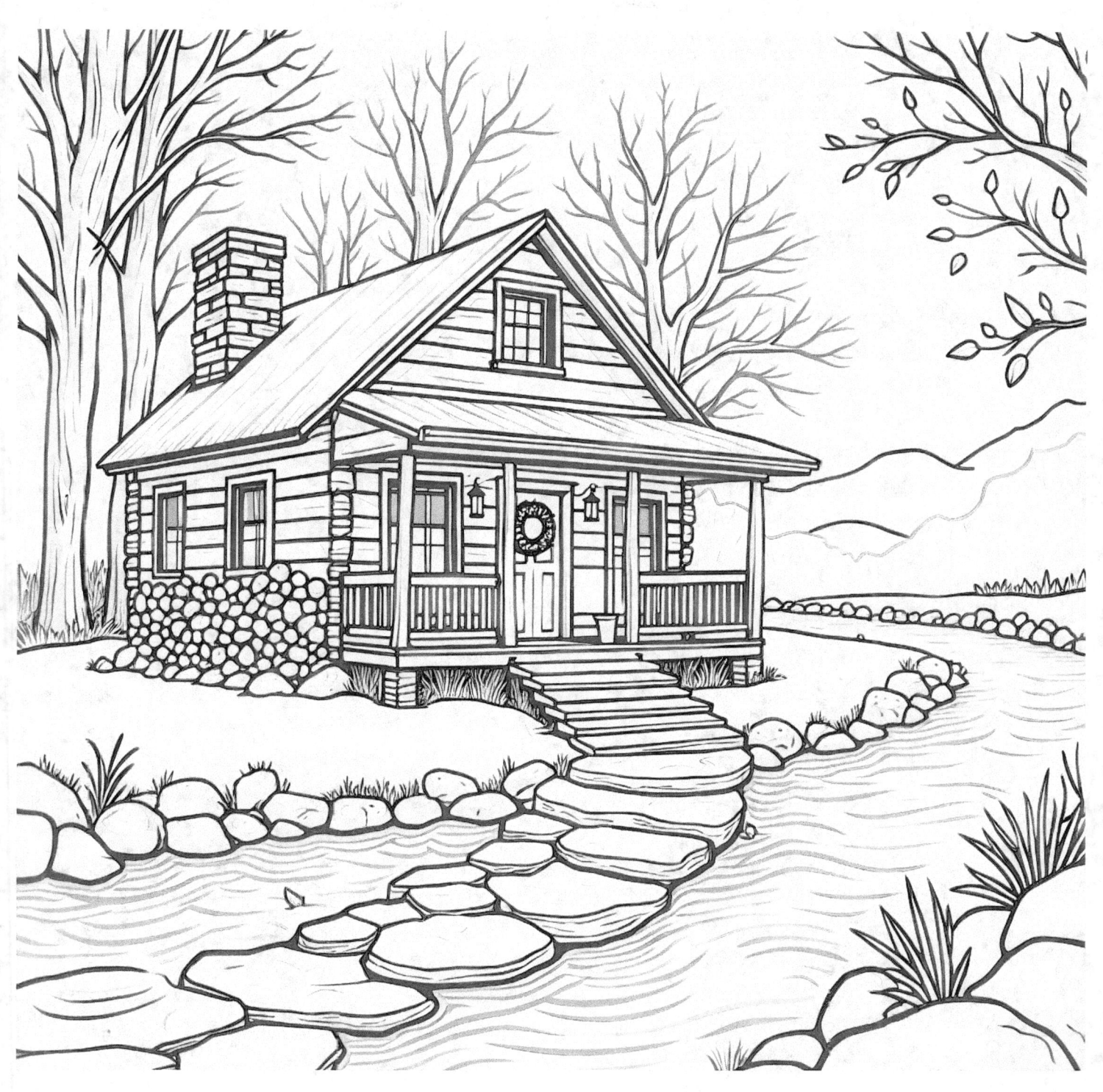

www.ingramcontent.com/pod-product-compliance
Lightning Source LLC
Chambersburg PA
CBHW082138290526
45794CB00008B/3084